Señora Ines; or, The American volunteers, a tale of the Mexican war

A S St. Clair

Nabu Public Domain Reprints:

You are holding a reproduction of an original work published before 1923 that is in the public domain in the United States of America, and possibly other countries. You may freely copy and distribute this work as no entity (individual or corporate) has a copyright on the body of the work. This book may contain prior copyright references, and library stamps (as most of these works were scanned from library copies). These have been scanned and retained as part of the historical artifact.

This book may have occasional imperfections such as missing or blurred pages, poor pictures, errant marks, etc. that were either part of the original artifact, or were introduced by the scanning process. We believe this work is culturally important, and despite the imperfections, have elected to bring it back into print as part of our continuing commitment to the preservation of printed works worldwide. We appreciate your understanding of the imperfections in the preservation process, and hope you enjoy this valuable book.

SENORA INES:

OR,

THE AMERICAN VOLUNTEERS.

A Tale of the Mexican War.

BY A. S. ST. CLAIR.

'' Tis past! The sultry tyrant of the south
Has spent his short-lived rage; more grateful hours
Move silent on.'   BARBAULD.

BOSTON:
PUBLISHED BY F. GLEASON,
AT THE FLAG OF OUR UNION OFFICE,
CORNER OF COURT AND TREMONT STREETS.

FIC
CLAIR

Entered, according to Act of Congress, in the year 1848,
BY F. GLEASON,
In the Clerk's Office of the District Court of Massachusetts.

SEÑORA INES.

CHAPTER I.

Who does not remember Friday, the 10th of July, 1846. The heat of that day fell with scathing effect upon the gay city of New-Orleans. As the sun rose above the horizon, its first rays seemed to cast a burning veil over the city, which, as it ascended higher in the blue ether, and gained the meridian, became absolutely intolerable, suspending all business in the streets, and forcing the residents of the crescent city to retreat under cover, with few exceptions; and those melting beneath the sun's fierce beams, were taken home to bear the penalty of their temerity by almost immediate death.

But those who were sitting in their own splendid mansions, surrounded by all the luxuries of wealth, received not a breath of air to cool the fevered brow; but were sitting listlessly endeavoring to kill time by some trifling employment, or walking back and forth from room to room, in the impatient hope of inhaling a breath of what was not to be gained.

Having lingered through many hours in the delusive hope of a change in the atmosphere, the impatient watchers observed a small black cloud rising in the west, which spread rapidly, occasionally emitting from its dark bosom brilliant flashes of lightning, followed by hoarse peals of thunder, and in the space of five minutes it had covered the heavens like a pall; and the rain began to descend in torrents, while the vivid lightning, and menacing roll of the thunder, accompanied by violent wind, presenting such a contrast to the burning light, and almost death-like silence of a few moments before, struck an emotion of awe into every bosom. The storm continued unabated for half an hour, then gradually decreasing in violence, the clouds changing constantly, assumed every variety of fantastic form as moved by the wind, and in less than an hour from their first appearance, not a cloud was visible in the deep azure above. The cool breeze was playing its gambols in the street, rushing freely through every open window, thrown eagerly back for the welcome visitant, and imparting new life and strength wherever it penetrated.

In another hour the rattling wheels of the carmen were echoing through the streets, the market women had returned to their stalls, and were offering their choicest goods to view; while the principal streets were thronged with a gay multitude, eagerly rushing forth, invited by the refreshing coolness and purity of the air, to enjoy the evening hour. Business men stepped forth with renewed zeal. Here a gay party of ladies and gentlemen were walking and chatting in lively tones, there a party of gentlemen conversing upon grave subjects, others hurrying off to some convivial meeting, and still others sauntering about alone, or in groups of two or three.

Among the last mentioned were two young gentlemen, of distinguished appearance, who walked arm in arm, occasionally pausing to remark on some passer-by, and again absorbed in what seemed to be an interesting conversation.

Arthur Clifton was rather above the middle height, possessing a commanding, yet perfectly elegant form. His noble brow, shaded by locks of glossy brown, and the lofty expression of his deep blue eye, indicated the possession of cultivated intellect, and sensibility combined, while his countenance wore a composed and slightly grave expression.

Edward Stanley was the very reverse of his friend. His form was slight and graceful. His eyes piercing and black as night, were sparkling with gaiety and humor.

'Stanley,' said his friend, after a pause of some moments, in which he seemed to be resolving some important subject in his mind 'Stanley, I have nearly decided to join the army of General Taylor, as a volunteer in the struggle now going forward between our country and Mexico. What do you think of the project?'

'Think of it!' echoed Stanley, turning and gazing in his friend's face, to assure himself that he heard aright. '*you*, Clifton; you cannot be sincere in what you say. Rich, handsome, accomplished, the idol of the ladies, and envy of the men—impossible! It would not seem strange had I proposed such a thing, having neither of these qualities to recommend me to favor. I might perhaps gain a reputation for bravery, get promoted, and all that,' and his black eyes sparkled at the idea, ' or leave my bones under the sods of Mexico, which would be all the same to my *friends*,' emphasizing the last word with a bitter smile.

'My dear Edward, you wrong yourself and me, to give way to such fancies,' said Clifton, pressing his hand warmly. 'I have several times heard you speak with bitterness of your *friends*, and observed a shade of melancholy cross your features. We have vowed everlasting friendship for each other, and can you not trust the cause of those feelings to one, who, if not competent to advise, will at least sympathize with you?'

For a moment a shade almost of haughtiness crossed the brow of Stanley, but meeting the look of sincere affection beaming from the expressive eyes of his friend, he replied, 'It is a painful story, though soon told, and you shall have it, but not now—to-night at our hotel. And now tell me, Clifton, if you *really* intend going into Mexico, as you said but now, leave home, friends, and the luxury by which you are surrounded, to share the perils and hardships attendant upon the life of a soldier'

'Yes, I do intend it; but in speaking of the danger, you forget the glory, which will more than compensate for all that, you know,' said Clifton, with a smile

'Very true; but I am assured a person of your lofty mind and upright principle, would not embark in such an enterprise, without knowing his cause was just; and can you find a good reason for the invasion of a peaceable territory by our army?'

'Our government,' replied Clifton, 'thinks it has sufficient reason; indeed, thinks itself the aggrieved party. But let that be as it may, we have an army there, altogether too few to accomplish what they are required to do, and it is the duty of those who have remained at home to give them what support lies in their power. At least I feel it to be mine, to lend my feeble aid, not to the cause of invasion, but to the assistance of the handful of our countrymen who are in the midst of an enemy's country.'

'Then I go with you,' cried Stanley, after a moment's pause. 'There is something in the wild activity of a soldier's life, that strikes my fancy, and I will accompany you, as I have nothing to bind me more to one place than to another.'

'I do not wish to advise,' answered Arthur, 'though I will not deny that your decision gives me pleasure. There is a volunteer regiment forming here, in which I have been offered a captaincy, and if, as you said, you will join us, I will exert my influence to procure you a lieutenant's commission in the same company.'

'Nothing would please me more. I am sure I can trust in your superior judgment as to the right of the affair,' replied Stanley, with a gay smile. 'So now that is settled, let us walk on and pay our respects to those houris across the way,' at the same time directing Clifton's attention by a glance. 'If I mistake not, that is Mademoiselle Dupage, to whom you gave me an introduction the other day.' Clifton turned his eyes in the direction indicated, at the same time moving forward to join them.

While the friends are occupied in this movement, we will give a slight description of the ladies.

Mademoiselle Dupage was a pretty brunette, hair and eyes of jet, rosy lips continually wreathed in smiles, and eyes sparkling with volumes of mischief.

Her companion was about the middle height, possessing a form of perfect elegance and grace. Her hair was a rich glossy brown, eyes of the softest hazel, and her forehead, broad and white as the purest alabaster, gave evidence of intellect of an elevated order, while the expression of the mouth indicated firmness of character, combined with the soft and gentle affections. Though not strikingly handsome, she was formed to attract attention at the first glance. No one who gazed once upon her soul-lit countenance, but turned to look again, charmed by the variety and brilliancy of expression depicted there.

As the gentlemen approached, Miss Dupage threw back her veil, and shook hands cordially with Clifton, extending the tips of her fingers to Stanley with a graceful inclination.

'I am happy to see you out enjoying this delightful evening,' exclaimed Clifton. 'For some days past it has been almost impossible to move out, but this day of days has seemed to search the very blood in our veins, and turn one's breath into a flame of fire.'

'Yes,' replied Miss Dupage, 'and even now I think the blood in *some* veins is approaching a fever heat,' and her bright eyes sparkled with mischief, as she glanced at Stanley, who was gazing, with his soul in his eye, in the face of her friend.

He started, and colored, while the lady, at this remark of her friend, and noticing the look of undisguised admiration beaming from the eye of Stanley, blushed, and made a dignified motion to release her arm, and walk on alone.

'O, a thousand pardons,' cried the lively lady, resisting the motion, 'for not presenting you before; but I noticed the expressive language of Mr. Stanley's eyes, and could not think of interrupting anything so delightful. My dear friend, Miss Hereford.'

Both gentlemen bowed.

'Hereford!' cried Clifton, in surprise. 'Is it possible I have the pleasure of seeing the daughter of my respected friend, Joseph Hereford, of —— street.

'Thank you, I am indeed his daughter. It is but a week since I returned home, having been absent nearly a year.'

Clifton expressed his pleasure at the meeting, while Stanley crossed over, and taking his station at her side, gaily apologized for his unintentional rudeness, in allowing his eyes to follow the direction of his heart.

Miss Hereford listened to him with becoming politeness, and they were soon engaged in an animated conversation. Clifton and Miss Dupage walked on together, she chatting upon a variety of subjects, with all the giddy vivacity of a French girl.

'Well, Mr. Clifton,' she cried, after running on till she was weary upon other subjects, 'you see it is all over with your friend, poor fellow. I am sorry for him.'

Clifton smiled: 'Why sorry for him? he seems very happy just now.'

'Yes, but my friend Alice is *bien réservé* to all lover's vows. She has been absent three years at school, only spending the vacation at home, where she has been surrounded by a bevy of beaux. She seems to take pleasure in their society, but when they go so far as to propose, invariably, with a sweet smile, she says *no*.'

'Well,' answered Clifton, 'I hope that Stanley will not lose his senses entirely, or that the little wily god will befriend him, and plant *his* image direct in *her* heart.'

'Ah,' replied the lady, with a look of mock gravity, 'have you no fears for yourself? They say it is utterly impossible for a gentleman of any taste to spend one day in the society of the brilliant Miss Hereford, without falling in love directly. And though you have lived to the grave age of twenty eight, without losing your heart,' she continued, a roguish smile playing over her lips, 'yet, I will wager you this curl'—twisting one of her dark ringlets in her fingers—'against one of your own brown locks, that before you have known Alice a week, you will make a more desperate wish for yourself than you have just done for your friend.'

'I accept the wager,' said Clifton, with a smile as gay as her own. 'I assure you my heart is secure against all attacks from bright eyes and rosy cheeks.'

'Well, *nous verrons*; but here comes my father, who left us a few moments since, and Mr. Hereford with him.'

As the two gentlemen approached, Monsieur Dupage held out his hand to Clifton, with the remark, 'Devoted to the ladies this evening, I see.'

'Surely, I could not be better employed than at present,' bowing gallantly to the lady at his side.

'O, certainly not,' was the answer; 'but, ladies,' he continued, turning to them, 'I am in readiness to go home. Will you accompany me now, or do you prefer remaining still longer?'

'Whenever you please, sir,' was the reply, and the two ladies, with the doctor, walked homeward, Miss Hereford having spent a day or two with them, and her father walked on with our two friends.

Mr. Hereford was head of one of the principal mercantile firms in the city, possessing unbounded wealth, and a benevolence and taste, which enabled him to surround himself with all that was beautiful and rare, and gain for himself the heartfelt blessings of many a poor child of want. Alice, his eldest child, now about nineteen, had received every advantage that an accomplished education could add to a naturally splendid intellect. She possessed brilliant conversational powers, and an easy and graceful manner, which fascinated and charmed the listener. Her father almost idolized her, and could not, at this time, avoid speaking a parent's feelings in regard to her. Stanley felt she was too fascinating for his own peace of mind. Clifton expressed pleasure at meeting with his daughter, and hoped the friendship of Mr. Hereford, which he had the pleasure of enjoying, would enable him to become better acquainted with his family.

The old gentleman invited them both to his house saying:

'I have also a charming little niece, to whom I would like to present you. She is quite the reverse of my dear Alice in appearance and disposition, and is a perfect pet in our family.'

'Indeed, I think I have heard her mentioned, as being absent at school with your daughter.'

'The very same; a young Mexican senorita. She has been quite indisposed to-day, or she would have been out enjoying this delightful hour. But you must excuse me, gentlemen; I have an engagement with a friend, and must leave you.'

The friends bowed and passed on. Stanley remained silent, but his sparkling eye, and the heaving of his breast, told plainly to the experienced glance of his friend the state of his feelings.

Arthur sighed at the thought that those blissful hopes might so soon be changed to disappointment, and even as he gazed, the countenance of his friend underwent a change, his eyes lost their animation, and the deepest melancholy was painted on his features, while sigh after sigh agitated his breast. Noting these emotions, Clifton became lost in thought, and was roused from this mood by the appearance of a lady, who had just stepped out of a fashionable store, followed by a negro girl a few steps behind her. His eye followed her fairy form as she glided on before him, every motion full of infinite grace. He regarded her with a look of admiration, till, turning into a cross street, she disappeared.

As they reached the post-office, Clifton, who was anxiously expecting letters, stepped in, and Stanley, saying he had some business with his lawyer, and would meet him in an hour at their hotel, passed on.

When Clifton emerged from the office, his attention was aroused by shouts, and the rattling of carriage wheels. Hastening forward, he saw a span of horses, attached to a carriage, rushing down the street towards him, with the velocity of the wind. One after another attempted to stop them, but without success. As they approached Clifton, the carriage came in contact with a rude wagon, standing near, and with a crash overturned; and the harness giving way, the horses, with increased terror, flew along, to the infinite peril of all in the streets.

As they neared the corner where Clifton stood, he cast an eye back of him, and there, on a cross walk in the centre of the street, stood the lady who a few moments before had attracted his attention. She had turned her head for a moment, to reply to a lady who had accosted her from a window near, and utterly unconscious of the danger of her position, was smiling and waving her hand, when the negro girl, who was still near her, casting a look in the direction of the tumult which had just struck her ear, screamed in affright:

'O, missy Ines, come, come,' and with a terror that gave her speed, sprang to the side walk.

The lady's eyes followed those of her servant, and perceiving her perilous situation, attempted to move; but her limbs failed, and the very moment the horses dashed around the corner, unable longer to support her trembling form, with a faint shriek she fell on her knees, and with clasped hands and eyes upraised, seemed imploring a higher power than that of man to preserve her from this peril. Her bonnet had fallen off, and her raven tresses streaming in long curls upon her shoulders, and around her pale face, gave the latter a deathlike hue.

She was exceedingly beautiful, and at this moment formed a picture a painter would have coveted. But Clifton saw not this; he only felt that a fellow-creature was in danger, and springing forward with lightning speed, he caught the lady in his arms, from under the very hoofs of the trampling steeds; and the next instant was upon the walk, with his now insensible burden. At the same moment a severe but ill-judged blow from an enormous cane, held by some one near, caused the enraged animals to shy, simultaneous with Clifton's bound aside, placing him in the same danger as before.

Clasping the lady firmly in his left hand, with his right he seized the bits, and exerting the whole strength of his powerful arm, turned them violently aside; but as they passed he received a blow from the ironed hoof in the breast, which cast him lifeless to the ground, still clinging to the fair girl

The crowd gathered round, with difficulty released the lady from the clasped hand of Clifton. Having merely fainted from terror, she soon revived, and gazed wildly round with a bewildered air, till her eye falling on the motionless form before her, the truth flashed upon her, and with every feature convulsed with horror, she gasped, 'O gracious Heaven, he is killed, and it was to save me.'

Several gentlemen who were bending over Clifton, assured her there was still a motion of the heart; and he might yet be restored. Thanking them, she turned eagerly to one of the bystanders, dropped a piece of silver in his hand, and requested him to call a carriage. The instant it drove up, several gentlemen entered with the insensible body of the unknown, and the driver took a direction from the lady, who followed in another hack, after having sent for a physician.

On arriving at the door of her residence, she sprang out, motioned the men to follow, and passed through the hall into the drawing room, where a lady sat by a window, occupied in watching the frolics of a group of children, sporting on the green beneath.

Though forty years of age she appeared much younger, tall, and finely-formed, with an air of easy self-possession, indicative of familiarity with the higher walks of society. As the gentlemen deposited their burden on the sofa, the lady rose hastily, exclaiming, 'O, Ines, what, *what* has happened?' and then, obtaining a view of the features, turned to Ines in surprise, with a look of inquiry

A gentleman named Martin having given an explanation, the lady sent a servant for his master, and turned to assist the sufferer.

In a few moments the hall door was thrown open, and Doctor Dupage and servant entered, followed by Mr Hereford, for it was to his house and to the care of his lady that Clifton was brought. As the door opened, Ines bounded forward, and seizing the doctor's hand, cried:

'O, my dear sir, you can, you will surely restore him to life.'

He pressed her hand in reply, and advanced to the couch of the sufferer.

'Holy mother!' he exclaimed. 'Is it—can it be possible this is Arthur Clifton?—Not an hour ago I parted from him in perfect health and smiling with happiness.—When—how was this done?' turning a look of inquiry upon Mrs. Hereford, who, turning to Mr. Martin, begged him to explain what he had already related to her.

He complied, and turning to the doctor and Mr. Hereford, who stood gazing with sorrow and amazement upon the spectacle before him, related the incident, which bound up every other sense in that of listening.—Upon examination, a severe contusion on the back of the head and the marks of the hoofs in the breast were found. There was no fracture of the skull, but the blow upon the head had stunned him. He was placed in a warm bath, and the doctor opening a vein, after several trials, succeeded in starting the blood. At first it trickled but in drops, but soon flowed more freely, and in the course of an hour, the doctor had the satisfaction of seeing partial animation restored. He remained insensible to everything for hours; was very restless, and at times muttered incoherently. The doctor left him about midnight, after giving directions in regard to his charge, in the care of Mr Hereford and Mr. Martin, who volunteered to remain with him.

CHAPTER II.

'My heavy heart, the prophetess of woe,
Foretells some ill at hand.'

It was midnight, and the multitude that so lately thronged the streets, were wrapped in slumber. The noisy hum of voices had ceased. The free laugh and jocund song of gay promenaders had passed away, and the mantle of silence was thrown over the gay city. The majestic queen of night was sailing in proud beauty through the deep blue ether, her pure silvery radiance undimmed by a single cloud.

At this hour, in a large, splendidly furnished room in one of the principal hotels of ——— street, might be seen a young man, pacing back and forth with an appearance of the greatest agitation, occasionally pausing in his rapid course as if in deep thought, then hastening to the windows that overlooked the street, and casting an anxious eye over the moonlight scene without; then returning with as much haste, as if rapidity of motion could annihilate thought, throwing himself upon a sofa and murmuring to himself—'O,' cried he, 'why is he absent? Has he gone to spend the night with some friend? But, surely he *would not* without informing me of his intention. Never, since the commencement of our acquaintance, have we been separated one night. But no! my foreboding heart too truly divines that some fearful accident has befallen him. In one hour he was to have met me here; but how many long hours have glided away, and still he comes not.'

Stanley (for it was he), upon leaving Clifton, had proceeded directly to his attorney, and remained nearly an hour in consultation with him, then proceeding to their rooms, was surprised at not finding his friend already arrived. Taking up a book, he occupied himself for an hour; then sallied forth in search of him. Travelling one street after another, and calling at a variety of lounging rooms, without finding any trace of him, he suddenly decided to call at his friend Dupage, in the hope of finding him there. Ringing at the door, a servant in answer to his inquiry, said the doctor had been called away suddenly to visit a dying man. 'Then has not Mr. Clifton been here this evening?' The servant answered in the negative, and slowly turning away in disappointment, walked on with slow and desponding steps towards his hotel. But suddenly rousing from his pensive mood, he cried, 'What a fool I am, taking a wild goose chase around the the city, in search of one who will probably bestow upon me a hearty laugh for my pains. Let him stay away if he pleases, I will go home and sleep soundly in spite of him.' Accordingly, with this wise determination he ascended to his rooms; but they looked so lonely without the cheering presence of his friend, that all his old misgivings came over him, and pacing the floor with disordered steps, he gave vent to his feelings in words.

Edward Stanley, though still young, had seen much of the world's baseness, and had experienced its unfeeling fickleness in his own person. Having no near relative living; and going abroad immediately after leaving college, he had formed few acquaintances, deserving the name of friends. About two months since, only a short time after leaving college, he had happily saved the life of Clifton, who entangled with the trappings of his horse in crossing a stream, would inevitably have perished, had not Stanley with great difficulty rescued him. Clifton's ardent expressions of gratitude, joined to the repeated wish that their acquaintance so auspiciously commenced, might be ripened into sincere and lasting friendship by constant association, met a warm response in the bosom of Stanley, whose soul yearned for some object on which to pour out all the hoarded treasures of affection, so long pent up and driven back to their source, by the ingratitude and cruelty of those he had once regarded as friends. Clifton told him they were now in the vicinity of his residence, and gave him a pressing invitation to accompany him to the plantation, and spend a few days at least, where his mother would be most happy to entertain one to whom they owed so much. Stanley required little urging to accept so pleasing an offer. He said he had some business in New Orleans but it was not so pressing as to require immediate attention, and he would gladly spend a few days in the society of his new friend.

It was nearly sunset, when as they ascended a long hill, Clifton suddenly stopped and pointed to a splendid villa, about half a mile in advance, situated upon the shore of the Mississippi, exclaiming, 'There is my house.'

'And a delightful home it is,' said Stanley, his eye taking in the whole beauty of the scene. It was a large, old fashioned house, with a portico supported by enormous pillars in front. It was almost buried in a grove of trees, while the grounds were laid out in a tasteful style, being terraced down almost to the river's bank. As our gentlemen advanced at a rapid pace, the gate flew open at their entrance, and advancing up the long avenue, overshadowed by towering oaks, Clifton gave their horses in charge of a servant, and entering the house presented Stanley to his mother, with a brief relation of the circumstances attending their meeting. Mrs Clifton's cheek paled at the recital of her son's danger, and she expressed her lively gratitude to Stanley in the most fervent manner.

Mrs. Clifton was a fine looking woman, with easy, ladylike manners. An expression of calm serenity and perfect good nature pervaded every feature. She was, a native of Scotland. Her father, James Douglass, was the last of an ancient family, possessing unbounded wealth and pride of birth. He had but two children; James his eldest, was but twenty-two years of age when his father died, leaving his young sister Helen, then about sixteen, to his care. Soon after the death of Mr. Douglass, his son determined to gratify a long cherished wish of visiting the new world, and as Helen would not consent to remain behind, he turned his property into money, and taking with him all they wished for the present, placed the remainder in security, upon which he could draw at any time, and came over to our land of adventure. He spent several years in Philadelphia, where his lovely sister won the affections of all who approached her. At the age of eighteen, she gave her hand and heart to Mr. Clifton, a gentleman of good family and extensive property. Her brother now following his inclination for travelling, visited almost every place of interest, and at the end of four years married a lady of surpassing beauty and worth. She was of one of the oldest families in the country, though portionless. Mr. Douglass, being possessed of abundance himself, cared not for increase of wealth, and loved her for herself alone. He immediately became possessor of a splendid residence, and valuable plantation, about fifty miles from New Orleans, where Mr. Clifton soon followed, and retired upon the estate to which we have just introduced our readers, only five miles distant.

Here henceforth the two families remained, enjoying the delights of social intercourse until the cholera, that fearful scourge, passed through our country, when Mrs. Douglass and her three eldest children were swept away in one week. Her husband who worshipped her, followed broken hearted, leaving his only remaining child the little Helen, to the guardian care of Mr. Clifton, who at once adopted her into his family and heart. She was ever regarded with affection; but when Mrs. Clifton lost by the hand of death her only daughter, Helen took the place left vacant in her heart, and she grew up the pride and ornament of their house. Her engaging sweetness of disposition, the peculiar *naiveté* of her manners, and her devoted affection for her more than parents, and the adopted brother of her childhood, rendered her all that was amiable and lovely.

Mr. Clifton's death, four years previous to the opening of our tale, cast a gloom over the hitherto happy family. Mrs. Clifton had received several distinguished offers; but devoted to the love of her youth, declined them all, and lived happy in the society of her only son and niece. The latter at the time of Stanley's visit was absent at school.

As Mr. Stanley was a stranger in this part, Clifton took him on long excursions through the surrounding country; and when at home, they spent the time in entertaining conversation, in carrying out Mrs. Clifton's designs, about some new improvement of the grounds, or in taking a gay sail upon the broad bosom of the river; and in this way the time flew so rapidly that at the end of six weeks, Stanley could scarce realize he had been there as many days. But then he found that he must break the spell that bound him, and tear himself away. The very idea was painful, for he had become very much attached to Mrs. Clifton, who had indeed treated him as a son; and his friend he regarded as a dearly loved brother. They had reconciled him to a world that he almost hated, and directed his mind to a higher source than man for consolation. This was a direction in which his thoughts had seldom turned; and as he listened to the gentle, persuasive eloquence of Mrs. Clifton, and saw the effect of her faith in her conduct and uniform serenity of mind, a new world was opened to him. Therefore when he found that he must part with them, the thought cast a shade of melancholy over his mind. Every inducement was held forth to retain still longer, one in whose society they both delighted; but when he declared that business called him imperatively to the city, Clifton announced his intention of going with him, though it was but few weeks since he left there, which his friend heard with joy. At the time our story commences they had been in town but two weeks.

We must beg the reader's pardon for such a lengthy digression; but as poor Stanley's anxiety in regard to his friend was so great, we thought we would take part of the weary time off his hands, by an explanation of the commencement of so devoted a friendship.

But to return. Wearied at last with watching, he threw himself upon his couch, but not to sleep. Suspense, that most torturing of all earthly evils, was too racking to be endured with fortitude; and gladly did he hail the first approach of dawn. Soon after the first rays of the sun were visible, he stepped into the street, thinking the morning air would refresh him, and walked slowly on, musing upon the strange absence of his friend. When coming near the scene of last night's disaster, he heard several men talking together about an accident that had happened there. Eagerly grasping at anything that might give him intelligence of Arthur, he made some inquiries, and was immediately informed of what had happened. But they could neither tell him the gentleman's name nor where he was removed. Edward turned away, forcibly impressed with the idea that Clifton was the victim of the scene just related; and hastening to his hotel, was informed as he entered the hall that a man was awaiting him within. It was a servant of Mr. Hereford, sent to apprise him of the situation of his friend. He said Clifton was now delirious, and constantly raved of him. Stanley would scarcely give the man time to repeat his errand, but eagerly requested him to lead him to the side of his friend. Jumping into a carriage they were in a few moments set down at Mr. Hereford's door. Entering the house, and requesting the servant to conduct him to Mr. Clifton, they passed through a room in which several ladies were sitting. Impatient to proceed, he scarcely noted who were in the room; but bowing slightly to the ladies, passed on. As they entered the sick room, Stanley saw Monsieur Dupage, who was standing by a table near the door, hand a cup to a fairy-like creature, who turning to the outstretched form of his friend upon a couch near, pressed the cup to his lips. But he put it away with his hand, and raising himself with a sudden effort upon his arm, cried as he gazed wildly around, 'Edward, dear Edward, why do you not come; have *you* too, deserted me?' Stanley sprung forward, and bending over his friend, exclaimed, 'O Arthur, I am here, your own Edward, your devoted brother.' Clifton looked eagerly in his face for a moment, and extended his hand as if to grasp him; but falling back with a groan, murmured, 'No, no, it was only an apparition; and like the rest, when I attempt to approach it, flies from me;' and with a deep sigh he closed his eyes.

Stanley threw himself upon his knees, and pressed the burning hand of his friend repeatedly to his lips and bosom; while the stifled sighs breathed over it, betrayed his intense emotion. Arthur seemed to notice that some one was in distress; and starting upright in bed, with one hand he grasped the bed clothes convulsively, and with the other seemed trying to push something from him. 'O!' cried he, with horror imprinted on every feature, 'O! she will be killed! I cannot save her! See, the hoofs are now raised to crush her to the earth! O, Father of mercies, protect her!' covering his face with his hands, as if to shut out the horrid sight, he fell back exhausted.

At a motion from the physician, Ines trembling with agitation, and her eyes streaming with tears, now approached, and said a few soothing words to him, which calmed his agony, and he swallowed the cordial which she again presented to his lips.

The doctor now drew Stanley gently away from the bedside, and explained to him all that had occurred. Edward questioned him earnestly in regard to his opinion of Clifton's danger, and he answered frankly, that 'nothing but the most assiduous attention could save him.'

'O, then,' cried Stanley, 'I will not leave him day or night; and you, doctor, with whose skill the whole city is ringing, will save him?'

'I will do all in my power,' he answered, 'and with the blessing of God on our efforts, he may be saved.'

'I suppose it is impossible to move him?' said Stanley, inquiringly.

'O, quite impossible, it would hasten his

dissolution; and beside, when he is in his raving fits, no one but the sweet Ines can soothe him.'

Stanley regarded the lady with a kind of painful admiration, for he could not forget that for her, his friend had so nearly lost his life.

Ines turned her eyes anxiously upon them, and approaching softly, said, ' surely sir, you have no intention of removing Mr. Clifton from here?'

The medical gentleman shook his head, and Stanley said something of the trouble it would occasion them.

' *Trouble*,' replied Ines, with a look of reproach, ' could you think it would be esteemed a trouble, when Mr. Clifton has claims upon my gratitude, which can never be repaid.'

' Pardon me, dear lady, I meant no offence; but he is my best, my dearest friend, and now, in his present state, I cannot leave him.'

' Certainly not, sir; I am confident my uncle will be most happy to welcome to his house an intimate friend of Mr. Clifton. But if Mr. Stanley wishes the assurance from his own lips—'

She was at the moment interrupted by the opening of the doors, and Mr. Hereford entered. He advanced directly to Mr. Stanley, and offering his hand, expressed pleasure at seeing him, at the same time begging him to consider his house his home as long as Mr. Clifton remained an invalid. Stanley expressed his thanks for this privilege, and Mr. Hereford, noticing that their friend was tranquil for a short time, requested the pleasure of presenting him to his lady.

Stanley seeming reluctant to leave his friend, the doctor said it would be much better to leave him quiet for a time; and they accordingly left the room together. Pausing a few moments before they descended the stairs, Stanley inquired if the lady whose life had been saved by his friend, was the niece he had mentioned the day before.

' She is indeed,' replied Mr. Hereford. ' About twenty-four years since, her father, Don Carlos De Montaldo, a Mexican of high birth, spent some months in the city of New York, my native place. Myself, and only sister Alice, orphaned at an early age, were received into the family of a widowed uncle, who having no children, adopted us as his own; where we received every advantage that wealth could bestow. Don Carlos became acquainted, and soon ardently attached to Alice, and offered his hand and heart for her acceptance.'

' One short week after the proposal, our beloved uncle was seized with a fit of apoplexy, which in a few hours terminated his life. We sincerely mourned his loss, for he had been to us a second father. On opening his will, it was found that we were left sole heirs of his immense property; which joined to our own patrimony, made an almost princely fortune.

' Montaldo remained another month in the city, and then my loved Alice accompanied him home as his bride. Having nothing to detain me longer in New York, I travelled a year or two; and then wishing to be as near as possible to my dear sister, I came to this city, and soon after led to the altar one who made me the happiest of men.

' As long as my sister lived, we exchanged occasional visits. I well remember the last time I saw her. I had spent a week with them, and noticed with uneasiness that her health was failing. She was pale and thin, and a slight though constant cough was preying upon her strength. Her husband looked upon these evidences of disease with apprehension, for he almost idolized her. She had but two children, the young Alphonso, then about fourteen, and Ines, four years younger. I did not know that she felt any alarm in regard to her health, till our parting; when gazing upon her children with melancholy tenderness, she said, " These dear ones, I fear, will soon be left without a mother's guiding care." Then endeavoring to look more cheerful, she continued, "But I do wrong, thus to cloud our parting hour with such desponding reflections. Adieu, dear brother, and should we never meet again on earth, let us live so that we may meet in a happier world, never more to part." She threw herself into her husband's arms, and I turned away, with emotions too deep to utter a word. Three months after I left Mexico, I received a letter announcing her death. Though certainly anticipated, I was deeply shocked by the news. I soon wrote to my brother-in-law, with a request that I might bring Ines here, where she could have every advantage of education, and should in every respect be treated as my own daughter; but he returned for answer that he could not summon resolution to part with her now, but perhaps sometime hence he might be able to do so.

'Two years after that I visited him. He was very melancholy, and seemed to live only in his children; but at my earnest entreaty, consented that Ines might accompany me home, his desire to act for her best interest overcoming his reluctance to part with her; but only on condition that she should visit him often, and on finishing her education, return to bless his home with her presence. She has been with us six years, and now I suppose her father will soon send for her; but she is dear to me as my own child, and the parting will be painful in the extreme. But forgive me, my dear sir, I have detained you here longer than I intended.

Stanley assured him he had listened with pleasure to his interesting narration; and they now proceeded to the sitting room, where Mrs. Hereford, her daughter, and Marie Dupage were sitting. To the former he was now presented, and having saluted the young ladies, took a seat offered him. The conversation was grave, mostly relating to the sad accident of the night before; and if Stanley was fascinated by the variety and brilliancy of Miss Hereford's conversation at their first meeting, he was now charmed by the lovely expression of regret and sympathy, beaming from every feature. The young ladies knew nothing of what had occurred, till this morning, when they rode out with Monsieur Dupage.

Even the pleasure of the ladies' society could not keep Stanley long from his friend; and he was just rising to return there, when the doctor entered. He told his daughter he was now in readiness to go home, and asked Miss Hereford if she would not return with them. She smiling turned to her mother, who said they could not spare her any longer at present. As they retired, Edward followed them to the door, and pressing the physician's hand, again entreated him to pay every attention to his friend; then ascending the stairs he tapped gently at the door of Clifton's room, and entered. He was lying in a kind of stupor, the same as when he left him.

Advancing to Ines, he said he would sit by his friend, and relieve her from such constant attendance. She thanked him, and repeating the directions left by the physician, said if Mr. Clifton again became raving, he would find her in the adjoining room. She then retired and left him alone with his thoughts, and his meditations were not of the most agreeable nature. He was alone in the wide world, had neither relative nor friend, who he believed would sincerely sympathize in his joys or sorrows, save him who lay before him. The meeting of the day before with Alice Hereford had opened a new train of feelings in his bosom. Ever strongly susceptible of beauty of mind and person, it was not singular that he should be dazzled by such pre-eminence in both; and finding her also possessed of sweetness and sensibility, he felt then, even upon so short an acquaintance, that the happiness of his future life was in her hands. He sighed bitterly as he thought how unavailing, how perfectly hopeless his passion must ever be. Poor in the possession of what the world denominates wealth, though rich in the treasures of mind and heart, yet how could he ever hope that the rich, the brilliant Miss Hereford, the admired of all admirers, would deign to look upon him with eyes of favor.

He did *not* hope, and he felt that the only way to retain his peace of mind was to banish her image from his thoughts. Impressed with this idea, he buried his face in the bed clothes, exclaiming:

'And should I lose *thee*, my friend, my brother, may the hour that closes *thy* life, be the last of mine.'

It might have been an hour after this, when Clifton awoke with a start, but not as his friend had hoped, with reason beaming from his eyes. He again commenced raving. He called upon his mother, his cousin, and Edward, alternately; then seemed to live over the scene he had so lately passed through, till his delirium became so violent, that Edward stepped to the door by which Ines had disappeared to call her. Her hand was on the lock, and she immediately approached, and after a long effort, succeeded in soothing her patient to partial quietude. Then Stanley stepped from the room, and after a few moments' consultation with Mr. Hereford, a messenger was sent to apprise Mrs. Clifton of the dangerous illness of her son.

It is needless to follow Clifton's disease through all its course. Monsieur Dupage attended him with all the solicitude of a father; and Stanley watched by him day and night with a brother's devotion, scarce leaving him to take sufficient rest to support nature; while the lovely Ines was ever near, gliding like a ministering angel around his couch, anticipating every want, and soothing him into tranquillity with her low, soft voice. Indeed the whole family seemed to vie with each other in paying those attentions gratitude prompted them to offer. On the third day the messenger sent to Mrs. Clifton returned; but came alone! He delivered a letter to Stanley, from Dr. Hunter, her family physician. He wrote that Mrs. Clifton was very ill indeed—having been seized with the pleurisy, to which she was subject. He dared not communicate to her the dreadful tidings of her son's danger; in the fear that it would endanger her life—and nothing but *her* extreme illness could prevent him in person, flying to the bedside of one, whom he regarded as a son. He said, 'he knew, of course, Mr. Stanley would secure the best medical skill in the city, to attend upon his friend; and besought him to write to him every day, and relieve his anxiety.'

On the morning of the fifth day, Clifton gradually sunk into a slumber, so deep, so deathlike, that the anxious watchers by his couch many times bent over him, apprehensive that life had indeed departed; but his faint and scarcely perceptible respiration proclaimed him still an inhabitant of earth. About ten, at evening, M. Dupage was sitting with his fingers pressed upon the feeble pulse of his friend. Stanley sat at his foot, his hand pressed upon his brow; and the muscles of his face working with suppressed emotion—while Ines, the untiring Ines, stood at this moment at his head, on the opposite side, pale as monumental marble, with her eyes fixed upon vacancy.

At this moment, Clifton drawing a deep sigh, opened his eyes! They were entirely divested of their feverish glare, and the light of reason darted from them, as he looked about in surprise.

M. Dupage motioned Edward (who at the first movement of his friend had sprung up) to resume his seat; and pressing his fingers on the lips of Clifton, who was just unclosing them, he said: 'My dear friend, you have been sick, and are now very weak, and if you desire to recover, you must not say a word at present.' Approaching with a draught, he desired his patient to swallow it. He obeyed, and almost immediately fell into a sweet and tranquil slumber, from which they hoped the happiest results.

CHAPTER III.

On the following morning Clifton awoke entirely free from fever, with his mind clear and calm. M. Dupage called early, happy to find that his hopes were realized, and Arthur might be pronounced out of danger. He was weak, so very weak that he was obliged to recline in perfect helplessness upon his couch. But the fearful delirium was removed, and his friends felt confident of his recovery. A letter containing the joyful tidings, was immediately despatched to Dr. Hunter.

M. Dupage now answered the eager inquiries of his friend, by detailing all that had occurred since the moment of his fall.

'But, my mother! dear sir, why is she not here? did you not send for her?'

This was explained to him, and also that a letter had arrived that morning, saying that she was now out of danger. Clifton's extreme anxiety about his mother being somewhat relieved by this intelligence, he asked permission to see his kind friends, that he might thank them for the trouble he had occasioned them. But the doctor would not allow that.

'Wait another day,' he said, 'till you gain sufficient strength to support the exertion. It is absolutely necessary you should remain quiet! Mr. Stanley will set by you, and he must remember, that much conversation will only retard your recovery—and therefore avoid it.'

As M. Dupage left the room, Clifton warmly pressing the hand of his friend, said —'I may at least have the privilege of expressing my love and gratitude to *you*, O Edward! no brother could have watched over me more devotedly; and as a beloved brother I shall ever regard you.'

Stanley returned the pressure. 'O my friend,' he cried, ' the whole pleasure of my life consists in the enjoyment of your friendship—and now that you are spared to me I will be happy.

Though Clifton was not allowed to converse, yet his mind was active. He felt the most sincere thankfulness to that Providence who had preserved him through so much danger; and breathed a fervent prayer to Heaven, that he might ever remember from whence came all the blessings which were showered upon him. The devoted affection of Stanley dwelt upon his mind—and he determined to discover if possible the cause of that sadness, which often displaced the natural joyousness of his spirits, and if in his power, relieve it. Then the image of Ines de Montaldo flitted before his vision; he thought of her as he saw her in the street, when he sprang to her rescue—and again the glimpse of her agitated countenance, when he first opened his eyes from that deathlike torpor in which his senses were buried, seemed fixed in his memory.

The next morning when the seal was taken from his lips, Clifton reminded Monsieur Dupage of his promise the previous day.

'Ah,' cried the doctor, laughingly, 'I see you are eager to make the acquaintance of your beautiful nurse—and well you may be, for she has watched over you with the care of a sister. Indeed, she and our friend here,' turning to Stanley, ' have hardly slept since you entered the house.'

A smile and a tear contended for the mastery, as he listened to this speech. 'I shall never forget such kindness,' he exclaimed, 'but my dear Dupage, do not delay longer in granting my wishes.'

His friend immediately left the room, and Clifton desired Edward's assistance to raise and support him in bed.

In a few moments, Mrs. Hereford and Alice entered; approaching they expressed the warmest pleasure at the prospect of his recovery—and in reply to his animated acknowledgements, exclaimed, 'O, do not mention obligations, we are the obliged. You have nobly risked your life, to save one very dear to us, and for which we must ever feel the liveliest gratitude.'

Clifton's eyes now wandered over the room, in search of the dear one alluded to, but with a look of disappointment, he turned them upon Mrs. Hereford. Divining the meaning of the glance, she answered with a playful smile, 'Donna Ines will be here immediately.'

At that moment the door opened, and she entered, leaning upon the doctor's arm. As they approached, she left him, and advancing, eagerly exclaimed: 'Permit me to express a small part of the gratitude I owe you, for preserving my life, at such imminent risk of your own. O, sir, the most fervent blessings of my only parent will be bestowed upon the preserver of his child. Had you not done what, perhaps, none others in like circumstances would have attempted, I must inevitably have been crushed under those upraised hoofs.' Then covering her eyes with her hand, 'O!' she cried, 'that dreadful scene makes me shudder even now. I can never speak half my gratitude.'

'Dear lady,' answered Clifton, 'you owe me no gratitude, the act was involuntary. But I feel grateful to kind Providence which enabled me to save the life of one so very dear to her friends. But, my thanks are due to you, madam, for your kind watchfulness over me since I have been a troublesome invalid in this house.'

'What little it has been in my power to do,' cried Ines, blushing, and retreating to a seat, 'has been very slight, in return for so great a service.'

Clifton's eyes followed her, admiration speaking from every feature; but observing that she was embarrassed by his fixed gaze, he turned away and reclined in fatigue upon the pillows.

Mr. Hereford, who had before stolen in to offer his thanks and congratulations, now entered, and joined the happy group.

The considerate physician, however, soon reminded them that his patient needed repose; but he hoped in a few days he should be able to transport him to the parlor, where he could enjoy their society with more comfort. The company obeying his directions, our two *friends* were left alone.

Let us pass over an interval of eight days, and introduce our readers into Mr. Hereford's parlor, where a pleasant party were assembled—near a window which looked out upon a delightful garden, containing a variety of rare and splendid plants, sat Mrs. Hereford, employed upon a piece of embroidery.

Her daughter was sitting by a table covered with books—in the centre of which stood a vase of the rarest flowers, diffusing their rich perfume through the room. Stanley stood over her, slowly turning the leaves of a collection of splendid engravings which he had just obtained, and was now pointing out the beauties of different scenes.

Reclining on a sofa by an open window, our invalid was examining some new music; but his eyes often roamed to the face of Senora Ines, who sat a short distance from him, twining a wreath for a lovely girl who stood by her side. Mademoiselle Dupage was admiring her work, and twining her fingers in the ribbon of a guitar.

Suddenly Clifton handed Ines a piece of music, begging that she would oblige him by singing it. She took it, and glancing over it with a smile, took her guitar and running her fingers lightly over the strings, sang in a voice of melting sweetness, that sweet song,

'Though 'tis all but a dream, &c.'

As the last words died upon her lips, Clifton expressed his eager delight. 'That is a favorite of my dear cousin Helen,' said he. 'I have often listened to that song, as the rich tones of her voice floated in my ear, with the melodious accompaniment of that exquisite instrument—and thought nothing could exceed it.'

'Ah,' cried the lively Marie, 'I presume your raptures were not occasioned so much by the music, as the fair performer. If report speaks truth, that dear cousin Helen will soon become "*une chèrir epouse.*"'

'She is already dear to me as a sister,' he answered smiling. 'Her last term at school closes to-morrow; and unless my mother has informed her otherwise, she will look for me to accompany her home. It would give me great pleasure,' he continued, turning to Ines, 'to present her to you. I am confident you would be mutually pleased with each other. Indeed to my mind there is a striking resemblance between her and yourself.'

The heart of Ines palpitated forcibly at this remark—but summoned sufficient resolution to answer as politeness dictated.

Stanley, who had turned to listen, as the first strain of music fell upon his ear, now advanced and said: 'I've never had the pleasure of seeing Miss Douglass, but have often heard the gentlemen in the vicinity of her residence speak with rapture of her unequalled attractions. They described her as being beautiful as the creation of a dream—and sportive as a poet's fancy. The poor families around worshipped her very name—while her adopted mother and brother almost idolized her; and if our friend Clifton should endeavor to secure such loveliness as his own, none of us could blame, however we gentlemen might be disposed to *envy* him such happiness.'

'It is fortunate that you never met her,' exclaimed Marie, glancing mischievously at Miss Hereford, 'as you probably would have had neither eyes nor ears for any of the present company. Do you not think so, my dear Ines?'

'Assuredly,' she answered, raising her dark eyes with a smile. 'Mr. Stanley seems so much struck by the description of the lady, that should he meet her, Mr. Clifford might find a powerful rival in his friend.'

The gentleman smiled, and returned a sportive answer to this remark, while Miss Hereford raised her eyes to Edward's face—but meeting his in the same direction, averted them hastily, and busied herself in tearing in pieces a beautiful rose which she held in her fingers. At this moment, Mr. Hereford entered the room, and advancing to Clifton, presented him a letter; then turning to Ines, he said: 'And I have one for you too, my sweet niece, but I dread to know its contents, as I fear it will decree our parting.'

She received the letter, and excusing herself to the company, flew to her chamber to peruse it.

Mr. Hereford seeing that Arthur hesitated about opening his letter, said, 'the company would readily excuse him.' Bowing his thanks, he broke the seal and read. It was from his mother! saying that she was much better, but still quite feeble—and conjuring him if able to be carried home, to come to her immediately; as she could not feel assured of his safety, till convinced by his presence. She said, Doctor Hunter had gone to accompany Helen home, and she was quite alone. As Clifton communicated his mother's wishes, and said he must leave them the next day—every voice was raised in opposition, saying they were assured he would bring on a relapse by such exertion. He thanked them for their kind wishes, but remained firm in his resolution of going. Turning to Stanley, who stood gazing upon him, silent and melancholy, at the prospect of their separation, he extended his hand and said smiling: 'My dear friend, I have already been a great trouble to you, but will you add still more to the obligation, and take the charge of seeing me safe home?'

Edward advanced eagerly, 'O, indeed I shall be but too happy to be allowed the privilege.'

At this moment the door bell rung, and Monsieur Dupage was shown in. 'Well, my dear father,' cried Marie, running up to him, 'you are going to lose your troublesome patient here. His lady mother has sent an express command to take him home. I suppose she fears the attractions of some of us ladies may be sufficiently powerful to overcome the citadel of his heart!' Her father patted her cheek affectionately, and turning to Clifton, demanded if what she said was true. Being answered in the affirmative, he was going to express his decided disapprobation, but Arthur reading the intention in his look, cried, 'my dear friend, do not attempt to dissuade me from going home. The time passed on a sick bed has with me been beguiled of its weariness, by the agreeable society of friends; but with my dear mother, it must have passed on leaden wings, uncheered by the presence of either of her children. It is certainly but due to her, that I go immediately, even at the risk of very much fatigue.'

Finding it impossible to change his determination, the benevolent Dupage said no more.

The ever gay Marie repeated to him a dozen messages to his mother and Helen—then seeing that her father was waiting for her, she cried, 'well, I can stay no longer, so good-by, "*jusqu au revoir;*"' and shaking hands with him she flew from the room.

The next moment Ines returned; her friends glanced inquiringly into her face, and by the changes of her countenance, and tearful eyes, at once conjectured that they were soon to lose her.

Handing the letter to her uncle, she took her seat by Alice, and told her that in less than three weeks her brother would come to take her to her father. He wrote that he was very lonely; and nothing but her dear presence could restore him to cheerfulness. He also requested her to write her cousin to spend a year with them. This request she now made to her uncle, looking eagerly into his face, to catch the first look of consent. But he shook his head, with a smile, and a sigh, as he answered, 'no, no, we cannot part with both of you at one time. If it was not that your father's low spirits plead so strongly for your society, we could not think of your leaving us at all. But I suppose he has the first claim,' and he turned away to hide his emotion.

'When do you go, Senora?' asked Stanley.

'In less than three weeks!'

'*So soon!*' exclaimed Clifton, starting, and raising his eyes to her face. '*So soon*, and you may perhaps never return.'

'Probably not indeed!' she answered blushing, and turning away.

The conversation after this was anything but cheerful, and they separated early—Stanley going to their hotel to arrange everything for their journey on the morrow.

We will now follow Ines de Montaldo, for a few moments to her room. As she entered, her maid lighted a pair of lamps which stood upon the table, and remained standing, awaiting the pleasure of her mistress. Ines paced the room a few moments in seeming agitation; then recollecting herself, told the girl who was watching her attentively, that she would dispense with her services any farther, and she might go to her rest.

As she retired, Ines resumed her agitated walk, till pausing in front of a mirror, she glanced at the pale face reflected in it, and ejaculated: 'How inconsiderate have I been, thus to allow the image of this Clifton to be ever present in my thoughts. Might I not have known that he was in all probability attached to this lovely Helen, when he was constantly speaking in such high terms of her? And yet, I never imagined that what I felt for him, was anything but gratitude, till my friend Marie rallied him upon his penchant for his cousin! *Then*, I first learned my own heart, when a pang shot through it at the idea.

'O! weak, thoughtless girl! But I am punished! He goes to-morrow, and will never bestow a thought upon her, who will soon be so far away.' She threw herself into a chair, while the pearly tear-drops coursed slowly over her cheeks. Then, in spite of her determination to be miserable, the look he had several times cast upon her, made her heart beat faster, as she felt there was something beside indifference expressed in it.

'But why should I wish to inspire emotions in him, which can never end in happiness? O my father! why intent upon that hateful match? When so affectionate and kind in everything else—why doom your child to perfect misery, by forcing upon her a man she abhors? But O, there is something wrong in my heart! He says his peace of mind here and hereafter, depend upon my fulfilling a promise which he has solemnly sworn should not be broken! 'O merciful God!' she continued, falling on her knees, 'forgive my hesitation, and give me strength to do my duty, whatever that may be.' She rose more composed, and hurrying through her toilette, endeavored to seek forgetfulness in sleep.

The next morning, the family assembled with their guest, when Stanley entered, saying a carriage was at the door to take them to the boat. Clifton again repeated his thanks to his friends, for the attention he had received—and Ines advanced to repeat her soul's gratitude to her preserver.

Her lip quivered, and her face was paler than its wont, as she said: 'Mr. Clifton, it is probable we may never meet again, but my warmest prayers will ever be offered up for one who so truly merits them.'

Arthur pressed her hand a moment in both his own—then dropping it as suddenly, exclaimed: 'Think not, dear lady, this is our last meeting. I have nearly obtained a promise from Mr. Hereford, to bring this fair company, bowing to the ladies, to *La Grange Villa*, to spend a few days. But, even should I be disappointed in this hope, I shall most assuredly return to the city before you leave.

As he ceased speaking, he turned away, bowed to the rest—and leaning for support upon the arm of Stanley, proceeded slowly to the carriage. As they reached it, Mr. Dupage who was coming to take leave of his friend, stopped by his side.

'Ah! I am very happy to see you, doctor; we were going to drive to your house, but this is better.' And as he spoke, Clifton pressed a hundred dollar note in his hand.

The physician looked at it a moment, then returned it with a smile. 'You forget that I never take recompense for attendance upon the sick.'

'But, my dear sir, I do not consider myself an object of charity, and therefore must insist upon your taking it! If you cannot use it—there are surely enough about you, on whom to bestow charity'

'Possessing a fortune far exceeding my wants,' cried his friend, 'I assure you an addition to it would only be a trouble to me.' And turning away with a deep sigh, in a moment was out of sight.

'Ah!' thought Stanley, 'these men are consulting about the easiest means of throwing away their overbundance; while I have not sufficient for even the necessaries of life.'

As these thoughts passed through his mind, a torturing sigh burst from his bosom.

Clifton looked around to discover the meaning of that sigh—but his friend with a powerful effort recovered his cheerfulness—and they rode onward to the boat that was to waft them homeward.

CHAPTER IV.

*In struggling with misfortunes,
Lies the proof of virtue.*—SHAKSPEARE.

It was the third day after the incidents mentioned in the last chapter, that our *friends* were seated in the portico of La Grange Villa. Mrs. Clifton was reclining on a sofa, which had been rolled out to this delightful spot. Bare creeping vines wound round the pillars and over the roof, falling on every side in rich festoons, sparkling with flowers, which shed a grateful perfume upon the air. The sun was just sinking below the horizon, enveloped in a veil of burnished gold, while a train of white fleecy clouds, floating modestly at a distance, seemed waiting his majesty's pleasure, to attend upon his nightly slumbers. The broad bosom of the river was dotted here and there with sails, while a noble steamer was ploughing its way majestically through the waves.

Our friends had been for some time expatiating upon the splendors of the evening, when Clifton, turning his eyes up the road, exclaimed in delight, 'Here they come! dear, dear Ellen!' and starting up would have flown to meet her. but falling back in his seat, he cried with a smile, 'I believe I am *not* a very nimble pedestrian just now.' Half a dozen servants, lounging about the grounds, heard his voice, and screaming, 'O, Missy Helen has come!' started off, each doing his best to first reach and open the gate for their dear young mistress.

As the carriage rolled up the avenue, and paused just in front of our party, a gentleman opening the door stepped out, and the next instance, almost without assistance, a young lady alighted upon the ground. Darting up the steps she threw her arms affectionately around Mrs. Clifton, and inquired eagerly about her health. 'My dear, dear mother!' she cried, 'I have come home now, never more to leave you;' then kissing her pale cheek, she turned with a smile full of happiness to Arthur, who, opening his arms, clasped her to his heart, and imprinted a brother's kiss on her glowing cheek. Rising from his arms, she first perceived Stanley, who had drawn back under the overhanging vines. Blushing and confused she extended her hand as Arthur presented his friend; but recovering in a moment, she answered his compliments with ease and grace. Doctor Hunter, after exchanging a few words of greeting with the gentlemen, took his leave, saying he would not interrupt so happy a party. Miss Douglass now sat down between her aunt and cousin, and listened with sparkling eyes to their expressions of affection, and joy at her return.

As Stanley gazed upon the happy trio, he thought of the sad contrast to his own lonely state; a stranger, and almost penniless. He envied them such felicity; but it was not such envy as would have blasted their pleasure, because he could not enjoy the same. O, no, the greatest enjoyment he could now expect would be in witnessing the happiness of his friends. As he gazed on Miss Douglass, he thought the half had not been told him of her exceeding loveliness. She was about the medium height; her form was slender and delicately proportioned; her hair of that peculiarly rich shade, the golden auburn, fell in natural ringlets upon a neck of snow. Her skin was of dazzling fairness, and so very transparent, that the small blue veins were clearly discernible. Her eyes, of heaven's own blue, flashed at one time with intellect and wit; at another, timidly, languidly looked out from beneath their long silken lashes; and when she smiled, innumerable graces played around her small, exquisitely formed mouth. When her features were at rest, she seemed perfectly beautiful; but when vivacity sparkled from her eyes, and animation lent a warmer hue to her cheek, she was perfectly bewitching.

As Stanley gazed upon this lovely being, he wondered how it was possible that Clifton could look upon her only as a sister; but that this *was* so, he was convinced, by his manner towards her. As our invalids were fearful of the evening air, they now proposed returning within the house. The conversation here became more connected and general, in which Stanley joined; and he now found that Helen's mind was as lovely as her person. But the fate of *his* heart was already decided, and even her varied charms could not win him from his allegiance to her who occupied his thoughts. In consideration of Helen's fatiguing journey the party separated early.

Clifton and his friend retired together. Their rooms were on the second floor, and looked out upon a delightful shrubbery, where the delicious orange and lemon were interspersed with various flowery shrubs. Drawing seats near the open windows, they gazed out upon the blue night vault, studded with myriads of stars, and listened to the low murmuring of the wind, sighing through the trees; until a soft and pleasing melancholy stole over their senses.

Suddenly Clifton turned to his friend. 'My dear Edward, what time more fitting than the present, to listen to the relation you promised me some time since?'

Stanley sat a few moments silent and sad; then rousing himself with an effort, he answered, 'It is indeed due to your noble friendship, to let you know who you have taken into your home, and treated as a brother. Nothing but pride, false pride perhaps you will deem it, has hitherto prevented my disclosing some events in my past life, which it is not very agreeable to recall.

'I was the only child of affectionate parents, who, though possessed of but small fortune, were sure of a welcome into the gayest circles of the fashionable world; yet retiring within themselves they found more sincere pleasure than they could ever enjoy when mingling with the giddy throng. I was but two years old when my father died; too young to realize the loss; and in two years my mother married again. My father, at his death, was just established in business, with a capital of twenty thousand dollars. This was placed in the funds to accumulate for my benefit, as my mother had a handsome annuity in her own right. My mother's husband, Mr. Melmoth, was one of the finest men the world ever produced. In the course of four years they were blessed with a son and daughter. We were constantly together, and our affection increased with our years. Our parents were very fond of us; and I never perceived that Mr. Melmoth treated me any less tenderly than he did his own children.

'I was sixteen years of age when my dear mother was carried off suddenly by a violent fever. I was in college at the time; and though I then felt her death severely, yet when I spent some time at home during a vacation, and missed her loved presence—knowing that she could never return to us—my heart was almost broken.

'The house was robed in gloom! My father confined himself at home, and refused all society; we united our efforts to cheer him; and at last were happy to see him aroused to exertion. He smiled upon our efforts, and, at least, in our presence, summoned cheerfulness to his countenance.

'My young brother, Francis, was a noble boy. He devoted most of his time to study, and was very young prepared for college. My sister Rose was a sweet playful little fairy, who twined herself around my heart, with the most endearing tenderness. She possessed a fragile constitution, and our friends often said, "she would not long be spared to us." I returned to college, and remained till within a few weeks of the period when I should attain my majority. The two last years Francis had been with me.

'About a year previous to this, my father had married a young lady of great beauty, but without fortune. On my first introduction to her, something in her face and manner made a disagreeable impression upon my mind. She flattered and fawned around her husband, but I could not dismiss the idea that she would bring misery into the house which had always been the seat of happiness.

'She seemed to dislike me too, as if suspecting my feelings towards her. There was a man who visited often at our house, whom she had introduced as her brother; and as such, he received a cordial welcome from my unsuspecting father. I remained at home but a few weeks, and then announced my resolution of going to Europe. Mr. Melmoth did not oppose it, but told me not to draw upon what had been placed in security for me, until I returned. He then presented me with a large sum in ready money, and authorized me to draw upon his banker for whatever I wished during my travels. My first impulse was to refuse this gift; but he said, "You have always been to me an affectionate son; and do not now refuse me the pleasure of acting like a father; beside, the remains of the fortune your dear mother brought me, cannot be better appropriated."

'I could not refuse and wound his feelings, and therefore accepted it. I took a tender leave of my dear sister, and noble brother, and left my country for a far distant land.

'I will pass over four years, during which I remained abroad. I had heard often from all the dear ones at home, till the last year of my absence. I wrote repeatedly after that, but received no answers. In despair, I wrote to my father's attorney, whom I had reason to believe, was warmly attached to the family; but too impatient to await a reply, I set out in a week after. On arriving at New Orleans, I flew to my father's mansion; but judge of my horror, when his wife met me in the hall, and in reply to my inquiries for him, presented her pretended brother as her husband. She then assuming a look of sorrow, told me that my father, brother, sister, were *all dead;* that my sister died some months since, and my father and brother within a few weeks.

'"And *you*, madam, have married again in such indecent haste!" My surprise and contempt of her conduct forced this remark from me, even in the first burst of my grief.

'Provoked by my words and looks, she taunted me with the disgrace which had fallen upon my family. She said my father had become a perfect *inebriate*, and had cut off his children without a dollar, making a will entirely in *her* favor; that my brother had left college, and when his father refused him anything more to support his extravagances, had taken to gambling; and being reduced to distress, had claimed and received my fortune, by assuming my name, and had by gambling lost it all. That my sister, before she died, but *here* she paused, as the expression of my eyes probably told her she was venturing too far.

'I had listened to her horrid account, with emotions that paralyzed every faculty; but when she mentioned my *sister*, as one who had assisted in bringing disgrace upon me— an angel, whose name from every other tongue was *purity* itself— my indignation burst all bounds, and had she said another word, though a woman, I believe I should have struck her to the earth. As soon as I gained sufficient command of my voice, I denied her allegations with vehemence and contempt; but she told me with perfect coolness that there was legal proof of her words; and she glanced at him she called her husband, who immediately disappeared.

'In a few moments he returned and handed me the will, which I found as she said, entirely in her favor, and regularly signed and attested by several witnesses. I took the names of the attorney and witnesses, telling her she might yet find herself unmasked to the world in her true character.

'She defied me to injure her, and said the reputation of my father and family was too well known in the city, and that I would only gain hisses and scorn for my trouble.

'Disdaining to exchange another word with one so contemptible, I rushed from the house. Proceeding instantly to Mr. Melmoth's attorney, imagine my disappointment when informed that he had departed for Europe, two weeks before, for his health. I spent a week in the city with the hopes of tracing this villany to its source, which I was confident would lead me back to my father's wife. But it was all of no avail; and the stories she had circulated met me at every turn, till in an agony of shame, grief, and disappointment, I fled from the city!

'Mr. Melmoth had a plantation about sixty miles from the city, and as the bank in which my patrimony was secured, was near it, I determined once more to visit it. On reaching the bank, I found what I had heard was but *too true!* My fortune had been drawn by some one in my name; and by the description, it was my brother. The receipt also was given in his hand, with *my* name attached. My mind was harassed and torn, by contending emotions, until I was almost distracted; but when I reached the plantation, and the old house servants crowded around me with exclamation of delighted surprise, each one showing his affection for me, in his own simple way, I felt that I was not yet entirely alone in the world. I could gain no information from them about the late events; they had only received the notice that their master and all his children, *myself* included, were dead; and that his wife was heir to all he possessed.

"'O!' cried the aged housekeeper, "it was a sad day for us, when your lady mother died; and then to think that sweet Miss Rose must go too; and *now all* gone but you!" and she commenced weeping violently, in which the rest united. I could bear no more, and springing up, ran from the house. At the same moment a servant brought a horse from the stable. It was one my brother had presented me as a birthday gift. The noble animal knew my voice, and answered to his name. I sprang upon his back, and waving my hand to the faithful servants, was out of sight in a moment.

'Here I was cast out into the world, my sole possession the noble steed I rode and a a few hundred dollars. I had been educated to no profession, and knew not how I was to live. Almost wild, I was spurring onward to flee from myself, when I met you, and to my joy I found there was one being on earth who would look upon me with kindness; and from your noble friendship I have derived all the happiness, that in the state of my mind, I could enjoy.' As he ended, Stanley pressed the hand of his friend warmly, while the expression of his eyes was eloquent of his feelings.

Clifton had listened to this recital with great interest. He truly sympathized with his friend, and now sat a few moments lost in thought; at last starting up, 'My dear Edward,' he cried, 'I am convinced from what you have told me, that a deep laid plan of villany has occasioned all this trouble; and as soon as I am able to return to the city, the case shall be placed in the hands of one who will ferret out every fact, and I doubt not, return good account of it.'

'I have already consulted a lawyer about it,' replied his friend, 'but he says it is useless to attempt it, without a larger amount of money than I—' here he paused, and a vivid color overspread his face.

Arthur interpreting his confusion, cried almost reproachfully, 'Have not you preserved, saved my life? and could you not expect so *small* a service from my gratitude? Do not say another word! It shall be as I say! I will take the entire management of the affair. And now let us to sleep.'

The next day, after dinner, Clifton told his friend he would like to see him alone a few moments. When they were seated, he said, 'I wish to ask a favor of you, a great favor, and I hope I may trust in your friendship to oblige me.'

'O, Arthur! can you ask such a question? Is there *anything* in my power that I would not do for you?'

'Well,' answered his friend, smilingly, 'I am glad to have no more trouble in gaining my wishes. I have a plantation, ten miles distant, the agent of which, I have some reason to suspect, has not acted honorably; and if *you* will accept this agency, which he has forfeited, you can scarcely imagine how much uneasiness it will remove from my mind. The salary will be a thousand dollars a year; not very large, certainly, but—'

'O, Arthur!' interrupted Stanley.

'Wait till you have heard all, before you form an opinion. Of course, you will have no trouble about that till we return from Mexico; and in the meantime we will have but one purse; nay, do not shake your head, when you recover your fortune you shall repay me.'

'O, my brother! after all it is but another name for a gift of charity. But I will act worthy of so noble a friend. I will accept with gratitude what I can never hope to repay.' He turned away to conceal his emotion, while Clifton stole gently from the room.

CHAPTER V.

*Mirth, music, friendship, love's propitious smile,
Chase every care, and calm a little while,
But why so short is love's delightful hour?*—CAMPBELL.

Two weeks have passed away, and we will return to Mr. Hereford's splendid mansion. A gentleman and lady were sitting alone in the parlor. There was a striking resemblance between them; the same dark hair and eyes; the same high forehead and pale complexion. The gentleman sat twining the flowing ringlets over his fingers, and looking in the lady's face.

'Ines, dear,' he said, smiling, ' you have not changed much since your last visit home. I think our father will call you his darling little fairy as much as ever.'

'I hope so, I am sure; and I hope you will both love me very much, for I assure you it is quite a sacrifice to leave this delightful place, for your barbarous country.'

'Take care, my dear, what you say, or our father will regret ever allowing you to leave us. You know he wishes you to take back your heart safe, and allow *him* to bestow it where he likes.'

Ines turned deadly pale, and clasping her brother's hand, she cried:

'O, Alphonso, will he force his only daughter to marry a man she detests—one with whom she must ever be miserable? Surely, if he loves me as he professes to do, he cannot doom ms to such wretchedness.'

Her brother pressed the hand he held in his, and looking earnestly in her face—

'Tell me,' he said, ' have you already given away your heart, that you are so averse to Zenovia?'

'My heart is safe, I assure you,' she cried, hastily, though her blushes and faltering voice contradicted the assertion, but ashamed of her momentary confusion, she continued, in a more composed voice:

'My father must have some motive for this urgency that he has not revealed to me; for, I have often heard him express dislike to this man's conduct. Do you not remember when you fell into the lake, that our father, who was not able himself to walk a step alone, used every entreaty to prevail upon Zenovia to plunge in to your rescue? Yet he could not summon courage to risk getting wet, to save the life of a friend, and merely hastened to the house to alarm the servants, while Henri plunged in, and when sinking the third time, drew you safe to land, and was himself taken out insensible. Do you not see in that one act more native nobility of soul than Zenovia ever possessed?'

'Henri is a noble boy, it is very true, and I have often thought he might be of noble birth, and by villany have been translated to his present position.'

After a pause of a moment, Ines continued:

'And compare that man with the gentleman, who at such imminent risk of his own life, saved me, *a perfect stranger*, from such a dreadful death, when *he* would only have thought by flight to save *himself* from the peril of such an encounter.'

'It *is* then as I feared,' cried Alphonso, gazing sorrowfully at her downcast and changing countenance, and turning away with a sigh, he retreated to a window. The next instant he returned, telling Ines that a lady and two gentlemen had just alighted from a carriage, and were approaching the house.

The next instant the door-bell rang, and a well-remembered voice inquired of the servant if the family were at home. Ines hesitated a moment whether to leave the room or remain, when the door opened and Clifton entered, followed by Stanley and Miss Douglass.

Arthur advanced, and taking Ines's hand, said:

'I have been fortunate, indeed, to arrive before you left. I very much feared we should be too late. Allow me to present my dear sister, Helen. She is already prepared to love one to whom I am under so much obligation.'

The young ladies embraced each other cordially; and Ines welcoming Stanley, turned to introduce her brother to her friends.

The rest of the family now came in, and the introductions over, the evening passed swiftly away. Each one exerted himself to please, and there was not one present but at least *appeared* happy. Alphonso de Montaldo had seen many beauties, but NEVER had charms so dazzling, so enchanting, met his view, as when he looked upon the lovely Helen. He many times drew a blush to her cheek, by the fixedness of his gaze. At the tea-table he committed twenty blunders, which created a general laugh at his expense, as they saw by the direction of his eyes what had occasioned them. He smiled gayly in answer to their jokes, promised to do better for the future, and then became as forgetful as before. We will not pretend to say what were the dreams of our friends that night, but we think some of them might have been more pleasant than usual.

Three days were all that Ines could be allowed to remain with her friends, as on the fourth a steamer was to leave for Vera Cruz, which they were to take. Clifton and his friends spent their mornings at their hotel, but the afternoons were passed at Mr. Hereford's. The evening of the third day Alice invited her friends to accompany them to their green-house, and give her their opinion upon some new plants she had just procured, and which she believed were very rare. After spending half an hour, admiring the beauty and perfume of this splendid collection of exotics, Clifton asked Ines in a low voice if she would walk a little longer, and show him the little arbor that she had said was her favorite retreat. Then drawing her arm within his own, he conducted her to one of the seats placed within this miniature summer-house.

Taking a seat by her, he mused a moment, then exclaimed, abruptly:

'You leave us to-morrow, Donna, to go where new scenes and associations await you, and will you sometimes think of those you leave behind?'

'I love my friends too well, Mr. Clifton, ever to forget them, though hundreds of miles may separate us.'

'May I not have the privilege of hoping,' said Clifton, 'that *I* shall not be deemed unworthy of a place in your remembrance?'

'Mr. Clifton must have a strange opinion of me,' cried Ines, 'if he supposes I could forget one who has so much claim upon my gratitude.'

'Gratitude!' ejaculated Arthur; 'is *that*, then, *all* that I may hope for? I fear I shall never be able to content myself with so cold a feeling.'

'Respect, esteem, then,' said the lady, in a voice that trembled slightly with agitation.

Clifton took her small, white hand, and pressing it to his lips, suddenly dropped upon one knee, and softly whispered:

'Ines, dear Ines, dare I tell you of the ardent love that has been growing in my heart, since I first saw you? Will you not deem me presumptuous to hope that my sincere affection may be returned?'

She was silent. She averted her face, while tears she could not repress started from her eyes.

'My sweet Ines,' cried Clifton, gazing into her averted eyes, and imprisoning still closer the hand she attempted to release, 'do you think me unworthy your love? Have I raised my hopes too high—to one who regards me with indifference?'

Ines struggling with her emotion, at last gained voice to say:

'O no, nothing of that. Do not think I could be so—'

She paused, then continued, hastily:

'Mr. Clifton, it is impossible that I can ever be yours. Before I ever saw you, my father had promised my hand to one of my own conntry.'

Clifton sprang to his feet at this announcement.

'Then you love another!' he cried. 'Before we ever met, you had given your heart into the possession of another.'

Ines started up.

'Love him!' she exclaimed. 'O, Clifton, I hate—I abhor him! You—you only can ever—'

She sunk into a seat, and covering her face with her hands, burst into tears.

Arthur took a seat by her side, and drawing her gently towards him, he whispered:

'Dearest, does this emotion say that I may hope the fervent love of my heart is returned? Can it be that such happiness is mine?'

And his eyes beamed with the blissful consciousness that the answer would be according to his wishes.

Ines hid her face on his shoulder, and sighed in a voice scarcely articulate:

'Dearest Arthur, I can never love any but you.'

Clifton pressed her trembling form to his breast, and raising her head, their lips met in one long, fervent kiss.

A few moments of bliss unutterable passed over our happy lovers, then Ines, releasing herself from his arms, looked in his face with tearful eyes, exclaiming:

'What will my father say, when he knows of this? He will call me disobedient, ungrateful.'

'My dear girl,' replied Arthur, 'your father cannot be so cruel as to insist upon giving your hand where you cannot bestow your heart; but, *should* he do so, remember, dearest, that a parent has no right to force the inclination of his child in that way, and from what I have heard of Don Carlos, I should think he would have no inclination to do so.'

'I have tried to think so,' answered the trembling girl; 'indeed, he *is* the kindest, most affectionate of fathers; but he has made a solemn vow, which he says, to save his own life, or even mine, he dare not break, and how can I disappoint him?'

'Then you will obey his unreasonable command, without an attempt to change his resolution, and without casting a thought upon the misery to which you doom him who adores you, and whom you have professed to regard?'

Ines raised her eyes with a look of tender

reproach; and clasping her hands tightly over her heart, to still its breath, she cried:

'O, Clifton, this is cruel!'

She attempted to rise and leave him, but her strength was not equal to the effort, and he fell back, pale and insensible. Clifton bent over her in agony; he called upon her by every endearing name to revive and bless him with the sound of her voice; but she heard him not. And flying to a fountain that sent up its sparkling waters a few feet from them, and laving a handkerchief in the pure element, he hastened back, and by its aid, in a few moments restored her to consciousness.

'Forgive me, dearest, loveliest of women!' he cried, throwing himself at her feet; 'forgive me for these hasty expressions—they were forced from me by the anguish of the moment.'

She pressed his hand and whispered:

'I have nothing to forgive. But, O, whatever may be my fate, do not again doubt my love, for *that* can never change.'

Arthur kissed the pearly drops from her cheek, and thanked her for the sweet assurance of her love, and then they talked with sadness of their parting on the morrow. He prayed her to tell her father of his passionate love for her, and entreat that he would not, by refusing consent to their union, make them both unhappy, and doom *his* whole future life to wretchedness, for he must indeed be miserable, if forever parted from her.

Our lovers, heedless of the time, sat nearly an hour, engaged in sweet converse, and had talked themselves into the belief that they must be happy, when the city clock tolling the hour of nine, startled them from their dream of bliss. Ines rose instantly, and giving Arthur her hand, to lead her to the house, said, smiling:

'Our friends will think we are lost, and be out in search of us.'

As they approached the house, they saw Alphonso coming to meet them.

'Ah, truants!' he cried, as he reached them; 'the house has been in a ferment for an hour, and I could not pacify the ladies, until I set out in search of the lost ones.'

Clifton replied, laughingly:

'We are able to take care of ourselves.'

Then opening the door for Ines, he continued, in a low whisper, as he pressed her hand:

'I will, if possible, gain over your brother to our cause, and then I am sure all will be as we wish.'

The two gentlemen turned back into the garden, and Ines tripped lightly up to her room. She knew there would be many difficulties to encounter, before she could hope to be united to the lord of her heart, if, indeed, that could ever be. But she was happy in spite of them, for she felt she was sincerely, ardently loved, and she was assured that neither time nor absence would change that affection. It was sometime before she thought of going below; at last, bathing her eyes and face in water, to remove any traces of tears, she descended to the parlor.

Helen asked her where she had been, and said, laughing:

'We were afraid you and Arthur had taken it into your heads to run away, and so sent your brother to look you up, and were just now trying to prevail upon Mr. Stanley to go in search of *him*. But where are the gentlemen? I think they show the ladies present great politeness.'

Ines returned some trifling reply, and at the moment the gentlemen entered. She stole a glance at them, and meeting a look of cheerful hope from the eye of Clifton, drew her ringlets over her face to conceal her blushes.

Helen's eyes had followed those of her cousin, and shaking her finger at him, while her merry eye was full of meaning, she cried:

'Ah, take care! I shall report you to your mother.'

'Ah,' answered Clifton, 'I hope my sweet sister will not have the heart to carry a *very* bad report about me.'

She answered him only by a mischievous glance, and turning away, commenced speaking to Ines of her regret at parting with one to whom she had become so much attached, during their short acquaintance.

It was late before our friends departed.—Stanley and Miss Douglass took leave of Ines and her brother that evening, as they were to leave early the next day; but Clifton, as he pressed her hand at parting, told Ines he should see her again.

The next morning a noble steamer lay at the dock, while all was bustle on board, preparatory to their departure. Carriages were constantly arriving, discharging their burden of passengers, and rolling away to give room to others. Just as the first bell rung from the boat, a splendid carriage drove up, and our Mexican friends, with Clifton, alighted from it, waving their last adieus to Mr. Hereford, who remained sitting in the vehicle, they proceeded on board and entered a private cabin, where Montaldo left them.

Ines had taken leave of her friends with the deepest sorrow, but *now* she was to undergo the agony of parting—perhaps forever—from one whom she loved better than her own life—one whom a cruel father might never again allow her to see.

As these thoughts passed through her mind, she threw herself into her lover's arms and sobbed out:

'O, if you was only going with us! to be near, to advise and console me in all the troubles I shall have to encounter from the persecution of that hated man.'

Arthur pressed her again and again to his heart, while he trembled so that he could with difficulty support her slight form.

'O, dearest!' he cried, his voice faltering with emotion, 'why must we part? Would to Heaven we had met under happier auspices,' pausing a moment. 'But I do wrong thus to depress our spirits at the moment of parting. You know, my love, your brother has promised to use his influence to put off all idea of your marriage for one year; surely, your father will not refuse so slight a favor as this; and before that time—I hope months before—I shall be with you to plead my own cause. Be firm and CONSTANT, my own betrothed bride, and the God in whom we trust will watch over and preserve you from danger, and enable us to meet again in happiness.'

At this moment the second bell rung, and Alphonso appeared at the door, saying:

'They are going to start immediately.'

Another warm embrace, a fervent kiss—'God bless you and have you in his holy keeping,' which burst from both their lips at once, and they parted. Clifton shook Montaldo's hand, and sprung to the shore. The next instant the steamer left the land, and went bounding gayly on her way, regardless of the heavy hearts she might be wafting afar from hope and happiness.

Our hero remained some minutes gazing after his friends, then drawing his hat over his eyes, he walked slowly back to the carriage.

'Forgive me for detaining you so long,' he said, as he took his seat by Mr. Hereford, and then the silence was unbroken, save by sighs, till Mr. Hereford alighted at his own door, and invited his friend to go in with him. Declining, however, he walked slowly on to his hotel. The next morning our friends left the city to join Mrs. Clifton, Stanley going home with his *friend*.

CHAPTER VI.

*Of joys departed, never to return,
How bitter the remembrance!*—BLAIR.

A FEW days after the incidents just related, Mr. Hereford was sitting in his private counting-room, making a few closing arrangements previous to leaving the city, when Monsieur Dupage was shown in.

'Ah, doctor, I am happy to see you. I am going to leave town immediately, to remove my family to a more secure residence during the sickly months.'

'True,' answered the doctor, 'it is not safe for them, yet I regret to lose your society. I have so few intimate friends, that your absence will add much to my loneliness.'

'Are you, then, going to remain during the visit of our southern scourge? You have escaped several years, but, though a physician, you may not always be so favored.— Why not leave now, and recruit your health, which I fear is failing?'

'O, no, my friend, I must remain. There may be many who will need my attention, who have not the means to reward a physician's care. I trust it is not unchristian impatience in me, but were it not for the sweet flower, who looks up to me for guidance and happiness, I could lay my head in the cold grave without a sigh. My angel wife awaits me in paradise; and my sweet babe I hope has joined her there, for I can find no trace of him in this lower world.'

The good doctor seemed to have forgotten that he was not alone, and was uttering to other ears what he had hitherto confined to his own breast.

His friend watched him with surprise, as he brushed tear after tear from his eyes. At last, breaking a silence which was becoming painful, he exclaimed:

'My dear Dupage, for six years we have been intimate friends, and though I never mentioned it to you before, I have often observed you sit silent and melancholy, in the gayest circles, as though unable to derive pleasure from such society; and now you speak of having lost a son, and yet of his fate being uncertain. If this is true, I beg you will confide in my friendship, and if the most unremitting efforts can relieve your mind, be assured no exertion shall be wanting.'

'Ah!' cried Monsieur Dupage, 'I have betrayed myself; but of what use is farther concealment? I shall never find my son, and cannot fulfil my vow to his sainted mother. But you must almost think me deranged, to talk in such a manner. I will give you a brief description of my past life, before you leave town, at any time when you are at leisure.'

'I am perfectly so at present, and am so deeply interested in the subject, that you will oblige me by giving it now.'

Then ringing a bell which stood on his desk, he told a man who entered to take care they were not interrupted. As he disappeared, Mr. Hereford turned to his friend, and signified his readiness to listen. After a few moments, Monsieur Dupage commenced:

'My father, the Marquis de la Croisy, was of noble family, and felt strongly that pride of birth which could not stoop to an alliance with an inferior. Early in life I became attached to a beautiful girl, who possessed every quality that my father could desire, but one. She was of good, but not noble birth, and he commanded me to forget her, and wed one of my own rank. This I could not do; and on leaving college, the lovely Marie became my wife.

'My father, on hearing it, disclaimed me entirely; but ashamed to see a son of his wanting the necessaries of life, he directed my mother to bestow upon me annually a sum sufficient to support us in comfort. During my last term at college, a gentleman calling himself Senor de Martino, from Mexico, saw and fell violently in love with Marie; and when he avowed his love, and met with a repulse, his disappointment and rage knew no bounds. He remained till all hope was destroyed, by our marriage, and then departed, telling Marie she would never prosper or be happy, for refusing *him* for a portionless boy. His prediction sometimes cast a shade over our happy home, but it soon passed away, and we thought no more of it.

'Four years passed swiftly away. My sweet Marie, and our little Henri, then about two years old, composed my little world of happiness. I was surrounded by none of the luxuries of my boyhood's home. We kept only two servants, but they were sufficient to do the business of our little household. I spent my time mostly at home, and now often look back upon those few years as the happiest period of my life. I often ask myself—

'"What is this world to us?
Its pomps, its pleasures, and its nonsense all
Who in each other clasp, whatever fair
High fancy forms, or lavish hearts can wish."

'About this time I received a letter from India. I had a bachelor uncle there, who was very eccentric. When he heard of my marriage and consequent banishment from home, he said I should never lose by it, and to reward my constancy to her I loved, he would make me his heir, and thus disappoint my father in his scheme of punishment. I never thought of it again, supposing it one of his strange fancies, till that letter came from his man of business. He said my uncle was dead, and after leaving legacies to his old servants, and a large sum for charitable purposes, he had left me, his favorite nephew, one hundred thousand pounds, on condition that I went in person to receive it.

'I communicated this intelligence to Marie, and saw by the deadly paleness of her countenance how much she dreaded the separation. It was several weeks before she could gain sufficient fortitude to bear our parting; and I was at times tempted to give up the fortune, and not leave her at all. But this I felt I had no right to do, and prepared to go; but it was with a foreboding heart that I kissed my dear ones, and turned again and again to gaze fondly upon them, as I rode slowly from the house. I had engaged a young lady, a friend of my wife, to remain with her during my absence.

'The ship that I sailed in was wrecked, and only myself and seven others escaped to land, losing everything but what we had on our persons. I had fortunately secured my papers and money about me. As soon as it was possible, I wrote to my dear Marie, as I feared she would hear of the shipwreck, and of course think I was lost also. After a very long and tedious journey, I reached India, and presenting my credentials to the solicitor, after going through all the formalities of law, I was at last put in possession of my uncle's fortune and title, that of Le Compte de Morinval.

'I immediately set out on my return, but rough weather rendered our passage long; and it was more than a year after I left my native land before I again stepped upon its shores. I had written repeatedly, but had not received a line from home. As I came within sight of the home which contained the dear ones, from whom I had so long been absent, I looked eagerly for the appearance of my Marie to welcome my return, but in vain.

'When I knocked, my old servant appeared at the door, and raising his hands and eyes, exclaimed.

'"Ah, Monsieur de la Croisy!"

'But instead of expressing joy at my return, he turned away and burst into tears. I sprung forward and caught him, crying.

'What does this mean? Quick—tell me what is the matter?

'But I could not wait for an answer. Hurrying onward, I passed through several rooms, and opened my wife's dressing-room, without meeting a person. There she sat, in a large easy chair, supported by pillows, pale as marble—her form thin and emaciated. She was robed in a dressing gown, scarcely whiter than her face. My heart contracted with agony, as I gazed on her. Her eyes were closed when I opened the door; but now turning her head, she rose with a sudden effort, and extending her arms, with a shriek of joy fell fainting on my bosom. Her young friend and nurse brought restoratives, while I bore her to a bed, and she soon recovered. It was a long time before either of us could speak. At last, throwing her arms around my neck, she sobbed:

'"I ought to be thankful that *this* great blessing is still left me; but, O Eugene, our Henri—our darling—is lost to us."

'Dead?' was the only word I could utter.

'"Ah, no!" she sobbed; "would that he was! But he is stolen—carried off—we know not where."

'My tongue seemed palsied; I could not speak; and I fixed my eyes in trembling horror upon her face. But she could not explain—she fell back completely exhausted upon the pillow, and motioned her friend to tell me all.

'"Ah, my dear sir," she commenced, 'it is a sad event. The dear child seemed failing in health, and his nurse took him to the sea-shore for a few weeks, in the hope that a change of air might have a good effect. It was not three weeks before Janet, the nurse, alighted from a carriage, and running into the house, fell on her knees before Madam de la Croisy, crying.

'O, dear lady, it was not my fault. I loved him as though he had been my own child. Our blessed lady is our witness; I would sooner have died than lost him.'

'"Your sweet Marie had listened to this raving in amazement, not being able to conjecture her meaning.

'"I was present, and begged her to explain what she meant: when she fell into an agony of sobs and lamentations, from which we learned that two days before she had been obliged to leave their lodgings, upon an errand which detained her for several hours, and left the little Henri in his cot asleep—Pierre, her husband, having promised to sit by him and watch his slumbers till she returned. When she came back, the child was not to be found, but her husband sat there as she left him, only he was fast asleep, and in a state of brutal intoxication.

'"She tried in vain to rouse him from his stupor; and leaving him, she flew through every room in the house, and then into the streets, wringing her hands and calling for her child. Some charitable people turned out to assist in looking for him; handbills were circulated and rewards offered—but all was of no avail; and in a state almost of distraction, she threw herself into a carriage and came here to tell the sad news.

'"My dear friend had listened, with hands clasped and tearless eyes, to this relation of her bereavement; but when it was closed, she fell to the floor, bereft of sense and motion. For many hours she fell from one fainting fit into another, and when at last these ceased, reason did not return. For four weeks she raved constantly of her husband and child, and it is only within three weeks that she has been slowly recovering."

'This is indeed horrible!' I cried; 'but have you no suspicions, to guide us to the perpetrators of this outrage?'

'"Ah, yes—not only suspicion, but certainty. Two weeks after you left home, Senor Martino came again to the place. He called here, and congratulated Marie on her happiness, said he had long since dismissed all unpleasant feelings towards her—praised the beauty of her child—and begged earnestly that he might be considered as a dear friend, who would do all in his power to serve her and hers. She thanked him, but said, coldly, that her husband had left her in such a situation that assistance from him, or any one else, was unnecessary.

'"A short time after he called again, apparently in the deepest sorrow, saying he had just received a letter from a friend in ——, giving an account of the wreck of the ship you sailed in; and saying that all on board perished. He came, as he said, to break the news more gently to her than another would have done. Even while he was there, a paper was brought in, which corroborated his account, in every particular. Then my dear friend sunk to the earth insensible; and as soon as restored to a sense of her misery, she went into strong convulsions, which continued through the night; and for many weeks her life was despaired of.

'"During her illness, Martino called often to inquire about her, and acted, indeed, like a friend. Receiving no letters from you, we were convinced that you were indeed lost; and your wife mourned for you, as dead.

'"Martino often called for some months, treating her with the most marked respect, and as tenderly as though she had been a sister; but I observed he would turn the conversation, when she spoke of you, and often praised the beauty and splendor of New Orleans, in America, and whispered a wish that he might be allowed to transport her there. At this remark, she turned upon him a look of haughtiness, which changed his manner instantly to that of a friend.

'"Shortly after he called and requested of Marie a private interview, but was refused.

'"I beg, dear lady," he cried, "that you will grant my wish, and if you desire it, I will never again intrude into your presence."

'"Marie looked provoked; but after a pause answered: 'Well, as you please.'

'"She led him into the ante-room beyond this, and requested me to come here, where I could hear every word that was uttered.— She then returned to the room, leaving the door slightly ajar.

'"Dear Marie!" he cried, as soon as she entered, "I have long sighed for this opportunity of declaring my fervent love for you; though I have been silent till now, my passion has burnt none the less intense. While you remain here, old scenes and associations will keep you constantly melancholy, and in delicate health. Accept the hand and heart of one who adores you; let me take you to new scenes and society, even to the new world; and you will soon recover health and the natural buoyancy of your spirits. And your sweet child, too, will have advantages which it is impossible for him to have here, in your circumstances. May I not hope that you will listen to my prayers?'

'"He took her hand and pressed it to his lips. Releasing her hand from his grasp, she answered:

'"Senor Martino, I feel obliged for your preference and offers, but I cannot accept them. My heart is in the grave of my husband, and I cannot cast aside the memory of him I first loved, and accept another in his place. I cannot bring another father over my child; and not for worlds would I leave a spot, rendered sacred by the loved presence in time past of him who only can *ever* occupy a place in this heart. Therefore, do not, I beg, ever mention the subject to me again."

'"She seemed to think the interview over, and was moving to the door. Martino threw himself at her feet, and besought her in the most impassioned language to have pity upon him—to think of his sufferings, and change her determination; but she checked him, saying, coldly:

'"I fear you would compel me to regret that I ever bestowed upon you my friendship."

'"He sprung to his feet at these words.

'"Indeed, proud madam!" he cried, bitterly; "you do well to speak thus harshly to me. It will nerve me on to my duty. And now mark well my words. You will never enjoy another day of happiness, while you have life. Sorrow and trouble will come upon you, from which there will be no escape. I *once loved you*, madam, but you *scorned* me, and I vowed revenge. I have never lost sight of you. I have had spies constantly on your movements. I was informed of your husband's intended absence, and repaired hither to complete my vengeance.

'"I made you believe he was dead. There, madam," and he threw down several letters, "I intercepted those. Your husband is still alive—he will return; but that will not bring you happiness. Farewell, madam; you will *remember* what I have said;" and he dashed out of the house like a madman.

'"I ran in, and found Marie standing in the centre of the room, her hands clasped, and her eyes strained in wild horror upon the retreating figure of that dreadful man.

'"She could not speak, but pointed to the letters. I snatched them up, and breaking open one of the latest date, read to her that you were indeed alive, and would soon start for home. At this joyful tidings she fell on her knees, murmuring:

'"He says I shall never be happy, but my dear, *dear* Eugene is alive, and coming home. O, I am already blessed beyond my hopes."

'"I stole gently out of the room, so as not to disturb her prayers; and *my* heart, also bounded for joy at the intelligence.

'"On the third day after, the news was brought us of Henri's loss, and at the same time this letter was taken from the office."

'She rose, and opening an escritoire, handed me a letter, which I opened, and read the following lines:

'"Madam—supposing you will be anxious for the fate of your child, I write this to let you know that your son is in good hands. I shall myself superintend and take the charge of his education; and for the *respect* I bear his parents, that education shall be worthy of them. His life shall be spent in the most degrading servitude, where his mind will be forced to grovel on a level with his low companions. He will be taught to believe himself the child of a licensed beggar, who sold him to a stranger for a trifle, to relieve him of the burden of supporting him. The son of the Count de Morinval, and heir apparent to the noble Marquisate de la Croisy, will assuredly be *proud* of his *parentage*. To assist you in the search you will probably institute, I would say, that Martino is not my name, nor Mexico my country."

'It was with great difficulty that I could control my emotions sufficiently to read through this insulting, this horribly aggravating epistle. I rose to my feet—my eyes flashing indignation—

'As sure as there is a God in heaven, or

might in this arm,' I exclaimed, 'that villain shall feel my vengeance!' and I started to rush from the house. My wife's sobs recalled me. I knelt by her side—pressed her hand convulsively to my heart.

'O, Marie!' I cried, 'how cruelly you have suffered, while I was not here to console and support you, under so much affliction; but, alas! what consolation is there. The cunning of that wretch will elude all our vigilance, and only despair remains.

'I will not, my dear friend, attempt to describe our sufferings. I had returned home with wealth, to surround us with every luxury the heart could desire; but we were childless, and what did we now care for wealth. In the course of a year, Marie presented to my arms a daughter. She was named for her mother, and since her death has been the world to me. For the first four months my dear wife exerted herself for her child, and I hoped she would recover her health; but, alas! vain hope. She faded away, and in little more than a year, sunk to her last rest, as gently as an infant to its slumbers.

'Had I known that my child was *dead*, his loss would almost have been forgotten, in anguish for the death of my idolized Marie. But to know that he was alive—fulfilling the wretched destiny marked out for him by that man of horror—added thorns to my misery.

'My father died a few months before this, and having forgiven my disobedience, left me a third part of his fortune. I had given my wife a promise that I would never cease my efforts to discover our child, while life continued; and placing my infant in my mother's charge, I commenced immediately the study of medicine, supposing I could better gain access to all ranks of society in that profession, than any other.

'But do not think I had been idle all this time. Every effort had been made to discover the villain, who had robbed me of my boy. I had sent emissaries to the United States, to Mexico, and through a great part of Europe. I had visited, and by persuasion, bribes, and threats, had endeavored to draw some information from Pierre, but he counterfeited innocence so perfectly, that I could say no more.

'Ten years passed away, in which I had gained a perfect knowledge of my profession, and had travelled much, always with one end in view. At this time, I heard that Pierre had been fatally wounded in an affray, and was taken to the police office. I went to him immediately, and with the certainty of death before him, he confessed that Martino had given him a heavy sum of money to give the child into his hands, and promised that he should not be injured, but that he would himself bring up the child in his own country. He said that after Martino took the babe, *he* had gone to the tavern to procure liquor, and drank to intoxication, so that he could not answer any questions. That the money he had received led him on from one wickedness to another, till now he had lost it all, and must end his life in a prison. He said his wife knew nothing of it—that she idolized the child, and had always been melancholy since she lost it.

'I could not look upon the wretch without horror; but in consideration of his repentance and confession, I gave directions to have him provided with every comfort, which was done, and in a short time he died.

'My mother and brother were now both dead, and the title and possessions fell to me. But the splendors of rank and wealth could not detain me from the cherished object of my life; and taking my young Marie, then a lovely girl of eleven, and the faithful Janet, I came here. Dropping my real name, and assuming that of Dupage, I hoped to elude the notice of Martino, if he was here.

'But, ah, my friend, my life has been spent in unavailing efforts, and I fear I shall never be blessed with the sight of my child. I never see a poor laborer passing along with slow and melancholy step but I eagerly examine his countenance, hoping to see the lineaments so dear to me. My dear Marie is all I have to console my sad hours. Can you wonder then, my friend, that I am unhappy —that the recollection of past happiness inspires such a regard for its loss?

"'Still unfortunate and vain'
To former joys recurring ever,
And turning all the past to pain.'"

'My dearest friend,' cried Mr. Hereford, who, by the humidity of his eyes, betrayed his sympathy, 'my efforts shall be united with yours, and I trust ere long your lamented son will yet be restored to your love; and if your amiable daughter will consent to accompany us, in our retirement for a few months, we shall indeed be happy. It will leave you still more lonely, my friend, but you might *lose her*, should she remain here.'

Monsieur Dupage, for by that name we shall still call him, pressed the hand of his friend, while the tears coursed slowly over his face. After a short time he gained composure to thank Mr. Hereford, and accept his offer about his daughter; and then walked home to prepare her for the journey. In a few days they left the city for a country seat, and the doctor felt more than ever his loneliness.

CHAPTER VII.

On stormy floods and carnage-covered fields,
The march-worn soldier mingles for the toil.—CAMPBELL.

By our reader's leave, we will now transport him, in fancy at least, to the Mexican city of Vera Cruz. The brave troops, under the command of the noble Scott, and his gallant generals, had been many days actively employed in digging trenches, and planting batteries, till on the evening of the 22d of March, having entirely surrounded the town, the order was given to commence bombarding the city—which was continued with little intermission for three days and nights. It was a sublime spectacle, particularly in the night, to watch the shells in their aerial flight till they struck within the city; to listen to the crash, as they pierced the roof, or wall of some building, carrying death and destruction before them. Then to witness the explosion lighting up the black expanse with a brilliant glare for a moment—then vanishing, and leaving tenfold darkness in its place.

But the inhabitants of the city were not the only recipients of these dangerous visitants. They returned the compliment in like manner, but happily with not very fatal effect. The Mexicans at last found they must surrender, or see their beautiful town completely destroyed; and finally, after some consultation, and treaty, the Americans took possession of the town and castle! And then the 'FLAG OF OUR UNION' floated proudly from the battlements—its broad folds waving gracefully out upon the morning breeze—and its appearance greeted, by the pealing thunder of hundreds of cannon: and the enlivening strains of numerous bands of music. A day or two after this, our *friends* retired together to their quarters, and throwing themselves into seats:

'Well, my friend,' cried Stanley, 'we are actually in the city of Vera Cruz; have conquered and taken possession of it by the most signal prowess; and are destined, I presume, to perform something still more brilliant, as we are to leave in a few days for Jalapa, *en route* for the city of Mexico. But you appear sad to night, what has occurred to depress your spirits?'

'You mistake, Edward, I am not low spirited! I was only musing upon various subjects. Do you not remember, it is just five months to day, since we left home, and parted from those we may never meet again? I often think of my dear mother's pale face, and quivering lip, as she entreated me to take care of myself, and remember that she and Helen would be alone in the world if I should fall. And then, the fervent blessing she called down from Heaven, upon her departing son, rests upon my mind; and even in the midst of carnage and death, it seems as though the influence of that prayer turned aside the weapon of destruction from my breast! And I was thinking of another thing he added with a smile. 'We are going immediately to Jalapa—and you know—' he paused.

'Ah yes, I know,' repeated his friend, laughing, ' I know the young Senora resides there, who brought away your heart to Mexico—and so, perforce you must follow to look it up.'

'Well, I hope I shall find it, safe and sound (or rather the one who has charge of it), and I shall not regret my long journey to obtain it.'

'I have another wish,' said Edward, 'and that is, that your Senor Zenovia may either break his neck, or fall into our hands a prisoner, in either case he would not be able to trouble you at present.'

'I thank you for your generous wish, my friend,' said Clifton, smiling. 'To tell the truth, I am quite impatient to get to Jalapa, where I hope to see Ines—unless her father spirits her away from fear of our army. I have sometimes thought he might make my serving against his countrymen an objection to giving me his daughter, or he may not have listened to her entreaties, and those of her brother—but have forced her long ere this to the arms of another. But this is folly,' he cried, coloring deeply, ' I do not deserve good fortune, if I always prophesy evil.'

Our *friends* sat a few moments silent and abstracted, then Clifton raising his eyes, suddenly exclaimed: ' My dear Edward, I think you have not played a very wise part, in one case at least.'

Stanley looked at him in surprise!

' I mean,' he continued, with a smile, ' that it was very strange you did not declare your sentiments to Miss Hereford, on your last visit, just before we left home.'

' Declare my sentiments to her,' cried his friend. ' What? throw myself at her feet, peniless as I am, and avow my love, only to be rejected with scorn and contempt, for daring to raise my eyes to one so far above me in fortune? No! I hope I have not lost all pride yet, that I could do so weak a thing. If I could have known she returned my ardent affection it would have been different.'

' I thought you *loved* her,' said Clifton, quietly.

' Love her?' cried his friend, ' I worship, I adore her. When in her presence, I live only in her smiles—and now, in her absence, her image is my constant companion.'

' I wish you would answer me two or three questions,' said Clifton, ' and I think I can prove what I have said. Could you think of uniting your fate with a girl who married you entirely for your fortune?'

' Of course not, if I ever hoped to be happy.'

' Then you do not consider yourself any less worthy of future happiness, for having unhappily lost a large fortune? and least of all, could you esteem a young lady who by looks and actions would evince her affection for you, before you even mentioned the subject; and had not even been more particularly attentive to her than to others of her sex?'

Stanley remained silent a moment—then looking up with an embarrassed air, he cried ' I see what you are about, my friend; you wish to condemn me from my own lips. I understand all you wish to convey, and believe you are not far from right. But tell me, Arthur, do you think it possible that Alice Hereford has honored me with any more regard than she would bestow upon any friend?'

Clifton met his friend's eyes riveted upon his face, with a look of such eager hope, that he could scarcely restrain an audible laugh; but with an effort he answered calmly, 'I think if you had avowed your regard for her, it is not only possible, but very probable that you might now feel quite different from what you do at present.'

He did not tell his friend that in a conversation with Miss Hereford, just before they left home, he had mentioned some incidents in Edward's life, and slightly touched upon an affection which he felt, but dared not avow in his circumstances. His look informed her of the object of that attachment, and he was convinced by her manner, that at least want of fortune did not lower Edward in her estimation. But being merely the result of his own observations, he would not mention it.

Our friends continued their conversation but a short time, and then retired to rest. Upon first leaving home, they had joined the invincible Taylor, and remained with him till Gen. Scott was appointed commander in chief; when most of the old hero's troops were drawn off to support *him*, our *friends* among the number. Captain Clifton and his lieutenant had by their gallantry and gentlemanly appearance, gained very many warm friends in the army, of both officers and men. As they were always together, they were styled the *friends*.

The army remained but a few days in Vera Cruz, and then resumed their march to the capital. On the 17th and 18th of April, occurred the battle of Cerro Gordo. All the operations of the battle covered several miles. A number of detachments of daring troops, under their gallant leaders, ascended the long and difficult slope of Cerro Gordo, which was the highest and steepest of all the enemy's works, exposed to destructive fire, pouring down upon them from the heights—and resolved on victory, drove the enemy from their works—planting the American flag where a few moments before floated the standard of the enemy.

Captain Clifton with his command was ordered round the hill, to attack a party of Mexicans, who held a position where, as they were concealed from view, they picked off many in the opposing ranks. When they found themselves discovered, and saw the force approaching to dislodge them, the first movement was to retreat; but their leader, a young officer of prepossessing appearance, by voice and gesture, incited them to stand by him. For a few moments they bore the shock of the assault firmly; but seeing their companions falling on every side, the remainder turned and fled with precipitation. Their leader called, remonstrated, and urged them to return—but in vain! 'Cowards,' he cried, curling his fine lip with scorn. 'Let them go—I will stand alone!'

At this moment, several blows were aimed at his head, one of which brought him to his knees. Then half a dozen swords were pointed at his breast. Unable to rise, he was attempting to parry their deadly thrusts, when Clifton springing from his horse with the speed of thought, dashed them aside, crying: 'Do not strike a fallen foe;' and stooping, he assisted the officer to rise.

'Sir,' exclaimed the young man, 'your noble conduct has conquered, I surrender to you;' and he presented his sword. But at the moment the eyes of the two officers met, and with an explanation of surprise each seized the other's hand.

It was Alphonso de Montaldo, whom Clifton had saved; and seeing that he was wounded and bleeding, he ordered him to be taken to a place of safety, and his wounds dressed, while himself returned to his station. By this time the hill was won, and a white flag appearing in the enemy's camp, after a short parley, Gen. la Vega, with his officers and men, laid down their arms. Santa Anna with his suite were now in full retreat for Jalapa, pursued by the greater part of the American army.

It was several hours before Clifton could be released from duty, to seek his *friend* (for Stanley was also wounded, and in the hospital). When they did meet, Montaldo held out his hand. 'I believe I must call you friend,' he said, smiling, 'even though I see you in the ranks of the enemy; and I wish to thank you for my life; as I should have thrown it away, had it not been for your interference.'

Clifton expressed his pleasure that he had been able to save the life of one he regarded so highly. Mutual inquiries now followed, about their respective friends. Alphonso told Clifton, 'that his father and sister were now at Jalapa, undecided whether to await the approach of the American army there, or fly to the capitol.' He said, Colonel Zenovia was in the army of Santa Anna, at the head of 1000 guerillas, and had probably retreated with his general. He also said, that his father had consented to postpone the marriage of Ines for one year from the time she reached home; on condition that at the expiration of that period she should give her hand to Zenovia. He confessed that the colonel was not a favorite with any of them—and he should be glad to have the match broken off, if such a thing was possible, without compromising his father. Ines had told him repeatedly, that she did not—could not—love him; but he had not sufficient manhood to give her up, though he certainly could have little hope of happiness, with a woman who could not, even *now*, conceal her dislike towards him.

'Do you think my friend,' said Clifton, 'that your father is so determined upon this affair, that he would oppose our attachment, was he not bound to Zenovia by a strong promise?'

'O, no, far from it! 'From what he has heard of you, I am convinced he is prepossessed in your favor; and I have even seen him shed tears, when listening to the account of your noble preservation of my sister. But it is that fearful vow! Why he made it I do not know, as he has never disclosed his motive; but as he *has* done so, he dare not break it. But do not despair! You are sure of my sister's affection, and something I am confident will yet happen to prevent so great a sacrifice.'

Clifton smiled. 'I am inclined to be of your opinion,' he cried, 'at least, it has always been my custom to look upon the bright side of events, rather than anticipate evil. But tell me, Montaldo, what are to be your future movements? You will be paroled, and allowed to go any where you like, except into the army again.'

'Indeed I have thought little about it,' replied Alphonso, 'not being aware of your general's intentions, with regard to his prisoners. My honor would of course prevent my again serving against you—but to stay in my own country, and sit idly by, witnessing the struggles of my countrymen, without one effort to assist them—I can *never* do! I think I will proceed to the United States. My mother was an American—and I have relations in New Orleans, who would probably welcome me, particularly as it would remove one from the forces of their enemy.

'I am glad,' said Clifton, 'that you think of doing so—but you will certainly visit home first?'

'Yes! as soon as I am able to ride, which I presume will be in a few days. I shall meet *you* there of course,' he said, with a merry glance into his face.

Arthur made no reply, but sat a few moments silent—then starting up and looking at his watch, he said: 'I regret to leave you —but I must stay no longer—we march in an hour—and I have much to attend to before that time. I hope you are comfortable here, and receive what attention is necessary for your wounds. I have endeavored to provide for that.'

'O yes, I have everything necessary; do not be at all uneasy about me. I shall rely upon your friendship, to see my father and sister, and quiet their anxiety for me, as I fear they have heard it mentioned that I have fallen.'

'I will certainly do as you wish,' replied Clifton; 'and now *good-by* for a few days only;' and with these words he left him.

Montaldo was surprised to see him in half an hour return. He approached the couch, and pressing the hand of his friend warmly, he cried, with a look of pleasure, 'I have just obtained permission of my commanding officer, to take you along with us. My friend Stanley is wounded, not severely—but so that he will be unable to sit his horse, and you will share his litter to the city. Will not this arrangement be more pleasant than to remain here?'

'My dear Clifton, you are ever thoughtful, ever kind. It will indeed be happiness to return so soon to the care of my friends; and to know that I owe such pleasure to you, will add still more to my gratitude.'

The captain now left him to complete his preparations—and in a few hours the last brigade was on its way to Jalapa. Leaving our *friends* to prosecute their march, we will precede them a few days into the city.

CHAPTER VIII.

*That best of fathers! how shall I discharge
The gratitude and duty which I owe to him?*—Cato.

The city of Jalapa is one of the most beautiful places in Mexico. It is situated in a picturesque valley, entirely surrounded by mountains. To the east, as far as the eye can reach, ranges of mountains rise one above another, till their summits, covered with perpetual snow, seem concealing their heads in the clouds of heaven. The rarest kinds of fruit are found here in abundance, and the salubrity of the climate renders it a delightful residence.

It was towards evening, a day or two previous to the incidents mentioned at the close of the last chapter, that a young lady was sitting alone in her dressing-room, in one of the most magnificent houses in the city. She sat before a small writing desk, with several open letters before her, which she seemed to have been perusing. Her raven tresses fell in long ringlets upon her neck, and around her pale face. Her right hand supported her head, while her left lay upon the desk before her. Upon her delicate front finger sparkled a diamond ring, upon which her dark eyes were fixed, with a mournful expression.

Raising it to her lips, she exclaimed, 'O, this is the only memento I have of his love, the memory of which has been my only comfort for many long months. And yet—not my only comfort—my father loves me. He is ever kind, ever indulgent. He anticipates my every wish, and is only happy when I am cheerful. I will be cheerful! It is due to his tenderness that I should exert myself to please him.'

She turned to the desk, and taking up one of the letters, read still again a page she had read probably fifty times before, in which her uncle Hereford (we take it for granted our readers have recognized Ines de Montaldo) had spoken of Clifton, as one 'he would be proud to call nephew, and who possessed as noble a heart as ever beat in man's bosom.' He said he thought him worthy of *her*, and *that* was as high encomium as he could pass upon him.

Her heart beat with exultation, at these praises of one whom she thought the most perfect of men. There was another item in her uncle's letter upon which her mind dwelt with interest. This was, that Clifton and Stanley had just left the week before, to join the army in Mexico.

She grew sad as she thought of all the dangers by which Arthur would be surrounded, and her heart sunk with apprehension, as she read the Mexican accounts of their enemy's loss, while she thought it hardly possible that he could escape, when so many brave beings were falling upon every side of him. She had heard that the American army was within a few days' march of Jalapa, and she knew that the Mexicans were determined to oppose their farther progress at Cerro Gordo. She had a dear brother also, in the army, and as she imagined those two loved beings, perhaps even now, opposing each other in deadly contest, she bowed her head upon her hands, and wept in agony.

A short time after this some one tapped gently at the door, and a gentleman of peculiarly benevolent appearance entered the room. He was perhaps fifty years of age. His complexion, and the contour of his features, proclaimed him a Mexican by birth. His form was still fine, and he had once been very handsome, but time and grief had written legible traces in his countenance.

Advancing to Ines, he threw his arm around her neck, and kissing her fondly, he said:

'Ah, my child, I see you are poring over those letters again. I believe I shall take them into my own possession, for they occupy too much of your time, when I am so covetous of your society. I really think I shall have to write to my brother, and let him know how fond you are of him.'

Ines blushed crimson, and placing the letters in her desk, moved her seat to her father's side, and pressing his hand in both hers, she looked up in his face with a smile of affection, as she said:

'O, I am truly blest, for I have the dearest and best of fathers.'

Don Carlos bent over his daughter, and gazed into her eyes, upturned to his, and beaming with love and tenderness, till, overcome with emotion, his head sunk upon her shoulder, and he murmured:

'What a treasure I possess in this sweet child, the dear representative of my sainted Alice.'

A few moments passed away, then wiping his dewy eyes, he rose.

'Come, my love,' he said, 'the carriage is ready, and we will ride for an hour on the Plaza.'

Ines immediately rang for her bonnet and shawl, and, taking her father's arm, descended to the carriage.

It was a lovely evening, and the Plaza was crowded with carriages, passing and re-passing each other in gay confusion. Occasionally, as they met, the fair occupants would exchange a few words of greeting, and talk gaily upon some lively subject, but generally the existing war was the theme, which, before this, they only dreaded at a distance; but now, it was approaching their very gates, and might bring death and suffering into their own households.

A carriage containing a gentleman and two ladies now rolled up, and stopping opposite Montaldo's, the gentleman inquired if he had heard any certain account of the expected battle, knowing that he had a son in the army. Don Carlos answered in the negative.

While the gentlemen were conversing, the young ladies were boasting of the valor of their countrymen.

'We shall surely gain a victory over these "barbarians of the north,"' cried one of them. 'Our troops have selected a very advantageous position, and they are resolved to keep it. Besides, their numbers are sufficient to crush their enemies at once. I have not the least fear of defeat. But why do you look so sad, senora? It is enough to bear ill fortune when it comes, without anticipating it.'

'You have no relative or dear friend engaged in this dreadful war,' replied Ines, 'or the knowledge of their danger would perhaps depress your spirits as much as it does mine.'

'Ah,' cried one of the girls, 'I had forgotten that you had a lover as well as a brother there. If the colonel knows how much alarm you experience for his safety, he will feel himself securely guarded, and dare anything to prove himself worthy of so much tenderness.' A slightly malicious glance from her eye closed this speech.

'O,' cried Ines, 'the colonel knows full well the extent of my interest in him, and I do not in the least doubt but he will take good care of himself.'

Her red lip curled with an expression of lofty contempt, as she spoke, and turning away, the carriages parted, and as they rolled off, one of the girls said to her sister:

'That Ines is an enigma to me. She never denies her engagement with Zenovia, and speaks of it as a thing of course, and yet how often I have noticed her eye flash, and her lip curl with scorn, when he was mentioned.'

'Ines,' said her father, as their carriage turned, and moved slowly towards home, 'I perceive, if the Americans gain the day, and their army enter this place, that you will be more than ever averse to this marriage with Zenovia. Mr. Clifton, if alive, will come here, and plead his affection against my wishes, and the result will be a clandestine union, leaving your father to bear the penalty of such conduct.'

'My dear sir, have I not given you a solemn promise, never to bestow my hand upon him without your consent, and do you distrust the truth of your child?'

'No, dearest, not your truth, but your firmness against the pleadings of one whom you love to enthusiasm. But to say nothing of that, if Zenovia should meet him here, and learn that he is the cause of your coldness to himself, a deadly meeting would be the consequence, of which I know you would regret to be the cause.'

Ines shuddered! He continued:

'Then why not at once consent to remove to Mexico, where we shall be spared all this? I have mentioned it before, but now, I see more than ever the necessity of the measure, both for your peace and my own.'

Ines threw herself upon his bosom, and with trembling eagerness cried:

'O do not take me away from here. If, as you say, the Americans defeat our countrymen, our dear Alphonso may be wounded, and brought in here: and surely we would not wish to be so far distant, and leave him to the care of strangers. And ah, my father, for months I have been looking forward to this time, and now that a few days only prevent our meeting, I cannot endure the idea of leaving the place without seeing Arthur. You will not go, dear father?'

Don Carlos cried, in an impatient tone: 'Foolish girl! you have no reflection, no care for the consequences. The present moment is all you heed. I did not think you so selfish!'

Ines was now sobbing as if her heart would break.

After a moment's silence her father pressed her to his breast, and kissing away the tears said, 'Forgive me, dearest! I was hasty. Dry your tears; I cannot bear to see you weep. We will remain here, and let events take their course. As you say, we shall be nearer our Alphonso should he need our attention.'

As they reached home, Don Carlos supported her up the steps, and again kissing her, said, 'Go to your room, my love, and compose your spirits, and be ready to welcome me with a smile when we meet again.'

Ines hurried to her chamber, and throwing off her hat, cast herself in a seat, to muse upon her father's last words—that he would let things take their course.

'Can it be,' she asked herself, 'that he means at last to consent to our happiness? Perhaps he feels that to keep such an oath when it would create so much misery, is more criminal than to break it, and thus conduce to the felicity of beings so dear to him.'

She knew not that she had any basis for her hopes, but hope she did, and when in an hour the door gently opened, she turned to meet her father, with sparkling eyes, and cheeks glowing with pleasure.

But it was not her father. A pleasant looking woman entered, and advancing to Inez, cried, as she looked in her face, 'I see something has happened to give my sweet child pleasure. May I not share her delight?'

Ines smiled. 'I do not know, indeed, my good Martha, that I have any more reason to be happy now, than yesterday at this time, but I believe my spirits are a little lighter. Perhaps we shall see dear Alphonso again in a few days. You know they have halted only a short distance from us, and whether they conquer or otherwise, he may soon return.'

'Yes, I know,' said Martha, with a quiet smile, 'and it is possible another person may be here as soon, either as a prisoner, or in the ranks of the conqueror.'

'O,' cried Ines, 'would that this cruel war was over, and peace might once more smile upon our unhappy land. But do you not think there will be bloodshed here, on their entrance?'

'O no,' replied Martha; 'they say the authorities are determined if necessary to give up the city, without an effort at defence, which they think perfectly useless if our army are defeated in the coming engagements.'

'I hope so,' said Ines; 'and now, dear Martha, we will go down and meet my father.'

Martha, as Ines called her, was a distant cousin of Madam de Montaldo. At the time of her marriage Martha was a widow, her husband having died a few months previous, leaving her destitute, and she gladly accepted an offer to accompany her cousin to Mexico. She had been in the family of Montaldo ever since, acting as nurse to the children and friend to the parents. She was well educated, and a pleasing companion.

On the death of Madam de Montaldo, she had charged Martha to watch over her orphan children, and teach them to worship God as their mother had done. Don Carlos never denied his wife any gratification, and the children were educated in the Protestant faith. They did not look to Martha as to a parent, but treated her with affectionate familiarity. Although Ines had been absent several years, on her return old habits came back with all their former force, and she loved her as well as ever.

The next day, the news spread through Jalapa like wildfire, that a hard battle had been fought, in which the Mexicans had been defeated, and they had retired to wait the morning for the renewal of hostilities. There were few eyes closed that night in the town, and towards morning the scattered troops under Santa Anna, came flying into the city. There was no time for rest, as they were hotly pursued by the enemy, and after half an hour's pause they again moved on.

It was very early in the morning, when loud and repeated knocks at Senor de Montaldo's door, alarmed the inmates. As the master of the house saw a man enter, his clothes disordered and dusty, his face pale and haggard, with every mark of fear and fatigue about his person, he cried in surprise:

'Why, Colonel Zenovia, you look as though you might have seen an army of ghosts, from the pallor of your countenance.'

'More probably an army of devils!' cried Zenovia, throwing himself into a seat. 'Cerro Gordo is taken, General La Vega and many thousand men are taken prisoners, and Santa Anna, with the remainder, are in full retreat for Mexico.'

After sitting a few moments he started up. 'My dear sir,' he said, 'this is no place for yourself and Ines. Will you not enter your carriage, and fly with us to Mexico? You shall be guarded safe to the city. Those barbarians will enter the town in a few hours, perhaps in one, and then I know not what may be your fate. Say, my dear sir, that you will go with us.'

'Impossible,' replied Don Carlos. 'Subject my tender child to the fatigues of accompanying a retreating army, warmly pursued by a victorious one? I should prefer remaining here, and trusting to the honor of our foes. But why not stay here, and guard us from danger, if you fear so much for us?'

'Stay here!' repeated Zenovia, and his face grew paler at the idea; 'indeed, that is out of the question. Stay here to meet those —to expose myself to—' He here paused, ashamed to finish the sentence.

At the moment Ines entered, and he turned to her with the same request, but she replied to it with even more firmness than her father had done. She begged to know 'if her brother was with him, or what had become of him?'

'I fear, my dear girl,' he answered with a sigh, 'that Alphonso has not escaped as well as many others. He was sent on rather a dangerous service, and his party was almost entirely cut off, or taken prisoners. One who escaped, said he saw his officer struck to the ground, and a dozen swords aimed at him. But they closed over him, and he could see no more.'

Senor de Montaldo turned deadly pale, and clasped his hands in anguish at this dreadful account, and Ines, with a shriek, fell back in a swoon. Her maids were called in to attend her, and Zenovia again resumed his flight, leaving the father and daughter to the indulgence of their grief.

In the course of a few hours the American army marched in, and took possession of the city, the authorities, and a committee of the principal citizens, waiting upon them and resigning the place into their protection.

Towards evening, Senor de Montaldo visited several officers to make inquiry about his son. He was received with politeness though he could gain no information whatever: but still he did not despair, as there was another division of the army not yet arrived, and he endeavored to comfort Ines with the possibility that he might have been taken prisoner, and if Clifton discovered him he would certainly provide for his safety. But in spite of this small comfort they passed a sleepless night.

It was nearly noon next day, before Ines rose from her couch, and descended to meet her father below. Seating herself in the open window, she reclined languidly in an easy chair, her mind occupied with surmises as to the fate of her loved brother, when her eye fell upon a small body of men approaching, in the United States uniform, with a wagon moving in their midst. She knew that the last division had arrived that morning, and supposed this to be some wounded soldiers whom they were conveying to the hospital, but how powerful were her emotions when the escort halted in front of the house, and the officer who commanded alighted from his horse, and bowing low to her, requested the privilege of bringing in two wounded officers.

The poor girl comprehended at once that her brother was here, and flew rather than ran to the door, where she met her father, and seizing his hand, without a word hurried him to the gate, which several soldiers were now entering, bearing a form upon their arms.

'My Alphonso, my noble boy,' cried Don Carlos, 'do I indeed see you alive once more?'

'Yes, my dear father, and with your presence, and my little Ines's nursing, I shall soon be well again. But be kind enough to pass on, my brave men. I have a friend in the wagon, for whom I have promised the hospitalities of my father's house.'

Ines looked eagerly at her brother: he understood her, and shaking his head, merely said 'Stanley.'

The men bore him to a room indicated by Ines, and returning, in a few moments placed Stanley upon a couch in another part of the same room, and then left the house.

Ines now dropped upon her knees by her brother's side. 'Tell me,' she cried, 'are not your wounds dangerous? Tell me, are you sure that care and affectionate nursing will restore you?'

'Yes, yes; dismiss your fears about me. I have no doubt that a few days will make me quite well again.'

Ines still remained kneeling by him. Several times she opened her lips to speak, but her words died in an inarticulate murmur. At last, unable longer to support her anxiety, the words 'tell me,' escaped her lips, accompanied by a look of imploring earnestness.

Alphonso glanced at her face, and seeing that she needed some reviving intelligence, pressed her hand as he said, '*He* is well and you may see him very soon.'

Ines bowed her head upon his hand for a moment, then rising, she touched a bell, and glided out of the room. Martha, who answered the bell, now entered the room, and kneeling by Alphonso, wept at the state in which she found him.

The young officers were not dangerously wounded, but rather weak from loss of blood. Every attention which love and friendship could devise, was bestowed upon them. Stanley was as well treated as though he had been in a father's rather than an enemy's house.

Senor de Montaldo and his daughter listened with very different emotions to Alphonso's account of Clifton's noble conduct towards him. The old gentleman, although he felt sincerely grateful, yet regretted that the circumstance would only increase the esteem of Ines, and as he noticed her sparkling eye and heaving bosom, his heart smote him that he must be the cause of sorrow to that gentle heart.

Alphonso said 'that Clifton's duties would not allow him to visit them during the day, but at evening he hoped to meet his friends here.'

The day passed slowly. It seemed to Ines that the sun did not move, but had taken up his abode upon the earth for a season. But the day did pass, as days always will while time lasts, and as evening approached, every sudden noise made her heart beat faster, every step brought the color of the rose to her cheek, and then blanched it to the hue of death. She was uneasy, company was a restraint, and she was glad when her father went out for an hour, attended by his confidential servant, or rather *protegé*, Henri Duvalle.

CHAPTER IX.

Lo, I am here to answer to your vows,
And be the meeting fortunate!—AKENSIDE.

When Captain Clifton entered the city of Jalapa, struck with admiration of its picturesque beauty, he was thankful that they had not been forced, by the hand of war, to deface its loveliness. He knew that it contained the only woman he ever loved; and his bosom swelled with impatience once more to hear her soft voice welcome him to her presence, and meet a glance of affection from those bright eyes, ever beaming with gentleness and hope. His duty kept him actively employed through the day, and when at evening he was released, and prepared for his visit to a mansion where his reception was rather doubtful, he was strangely excited, for one of his usual composure. Taking six of his men to guide him through the streets, as soon as they came within view of his destination, he dismissed them, to return to their quarters, and walked rapidly on. He had advanced but a few rods, when he heard the report of a pistol, and turning, he saw in an opposite street, several men struggling together, while oaths and execrations fell upon his ear. As well as he could discern by the light of the lamps, one man, in appearance a gentleman, was defending himself against three or four others, apparently of the lowest order. Following the first impulse of his nature, to help the distressed, Clifton bounded forward without reflecting upon the danger of throwing himself, alone, among a band of desperadoes.

The villains were too intent upon their object to notice his approach, and had just forced the gentleman to the ground; two of them searching his pockets, while the other held a dagger raised in a menacing position, in his hand.

With a single blow of his powerful arm, Clifton sent one of the ruffians reeling to the earth—then seizing another by the throat, he placed a pistol to the ear of the third, and commanded him, upon pain of immediate death, to rise instantly. The coward did as he was told, and the gentleman sprang to his feet, and advancing to the side of Clifton, prevented the trembling miscreant moving, by a firm grasp upon his collar. Seeing several men rapidly approaching, he called loudly for assistance; and Clifton, in a moment, had the satisfaction of being surrounded by his own men, who, on leaving him, had heard the pistol, and observing their captain change his course, had followed to assist, if necessary.

The ruffians made violent efforts to disengage themselves, but in vain; and they were secured and marched off. The gentleman thanked our hero in the warmest terms, and turning to a young man, who was just attempting to rise from the ground, and whom Clifton had not before seen, he said, as he raised him up, 'My poor Henri was struck down, in attempting to ward off a blow intended for me, but I hope you are not much hurt?' addressing his friend.

'I think not,' he answered; 'the blow upon my head stunned me for a moment, but I am well now.'

The old gentleman invited his champion to accompany him home. 'I see,' he said, 'from your dress, you are one of the army now in possession of this place. I will not indeed call you an enemy, you have performed the part of a friend.'

Arthur however declined his invitation, saying 'he was engaged this evening, but would be happy, at another time, to avail himself of his offer.'

'I regret much,' said the gentleman, 'that you will not go in, this evening, and receive the thanks of my family, as well as my own. But do let me see you soon. And may I not know the name of my preserver? My own is Montaldo.'

Clifton started in surprise, but in a moment recovering, he advanced to the young man, saying, 'I see, sir, that you are weak, and not able to walk alone; lean on my arm, and I will have the pleasure of calling for a moment, at least.'

Senor De Montaldo preceded them into the house, and Henri was placed upon a sofa. Clifton's athletic frame trembled as, turning, Don Carlos cried, 'My daughter—my dear Ines—welcome—and thank your father's preserver.' He was going on to explain, when, who can express his astonishment to see his daughter fall into the extended arms of the stranger. Understanding now *who* the stranger was, Don Carlos gazed at them a moment with a troubled look. At last approaching Henri, and saying a few words to him in a low voice, he rose, and they left the room together.

'My sweet, my lovely Ines,' whispered Clifton, as the door closed, 'I am blest, O, how blest, to meet you once more and know, that though we have been parted long, you have not forgotten me.'

'Forgotten! Ah, Clifton, what else have I had to think of these many long months? This dear pledge you slipped upon my finger at parting, my father says has occupied more of my attention than I have given to him. I heard that you were coming into Mexico, and the idea of your danger has been ever before me.'

'Did you not receive my letters?' cried Arthur; 'I have sent you several before and since I entered Mexico.'

'Then you *did* write to me!' she exclaimed. 'O, how could I doubt it? But when so many months passed away, and I received not a line from you, I sometimes feared—'

Arthur prevented her finishing the sentence by pressing his lips to her's. 'Do not give those ideas words, my love,' he said, 'you never should have doubted the constancy of your own Arthur, who loves you better than his own life. Never has a doubt of *your* faith entered *my* heart, although I knew your father would use every effort to banish me from your mind.'

The tears sprang to Ines's eyes in a moment, at these words. 'O, Arthur, forgive me,' she cried; 'if *ever* I distrusted you, it was but for a moment. O, never longer. It made me too unhappy.'

Clifton smiling, said, 'Well, take care that you do not doubt me again;' and he sealed the oblivion of her fault on her lips.

We will not attempt to repeat their conversation. It was of much greater interest to them than any one else, as lovers' conversations usually are; beside, it would be scarcely polite to play the eaves-dropper in such a delicate case.

It was quite late before Senor De Montaldo returned to the room, and when he did, it was with an expression of suffering in his countenance. Walking up to Clifton, he said, 'Senor, it seems to be your fate to be constantly placing me under renewed obligations. This is the third time that you have rendered my family the most essential service, and the gratitude of a life cannot reward you.'

'Ah, sir, you have it in your power to reward me far exceeding my services;' and Clifton pressed the hand of Ines to his lips.

Don Carlos looked grave as he replied, 'We will not speak of that subject at present, Senor. At another time I will explain all you wish to know in regard to that.'

These words, with the expression of his countenance, struck a chill to the heart of Clifton. It seemed to him they foreboded some cruel ruin to his hopes. And he drew her loved form still closer to him, as though his power could prevent their separation.

Senor De Montaldo remained a short time silent, then told Arthur that his son and Stanley would not see him to-night, as they were quite fatigued and had been carried to their rooms some hours before.

'Then I will return to-morrow,' he said, rising, and bowing. 'You mistake, my friend,' said Montaldo, laying his hand upon the other's arm. 'You will stay with us, certainly? I cannot consent that you should leave us to-night.'

Clifton thanked him, but was again moving towards the door, when he caught a beseeching look from Ines, which brought him back to her side, but too happy to be convinced that it was best to remain. The next morning Clifton visited the invalids, and found them both meditating an attempt to rise, saying, 'they were sick of confinement, and wished to enjoy the society of their friends below.' The captain reasoned calmly with them upon the folly of such a proceeding; and Stanley gave up at once, as he was never accustomed to dispute the wishes of his friend.

As Clifton left the room, he was met by Henri Duvalle, who told him the family awaited him in the breakfast room. Henri might have been, perhaps, twenty-two years of age. He was pale, though of dark complexion. An expression of sadness constantly dwelt upon his features, and Clifton read in the proud humility of his brow, that his soul was far above his station. His countenance seemed familiar to the captain; but where they had met he could not conjecture.

He mentioned this idea to his friends; and Ines said 'he often reminded her of Dr. Dupage.'

'Ah, surely,' answered Clifton, 'it must be this resemblance which struck me. But of course it is because they are of the same country, as I have often heard that Marie was all the child he had. Has this Henri been long in your family?' he added, turning to Don Carlos.

'About thirteen years,' said Montaldo. 'A friend of mine, while travelling in France, found him in the streets. His father, who was one of the lowest class, gave him to my friend for a trifle, and in pity to the child he brought him away from so unnatural a parent. Henri remained in his family several years, and he then placed him with me, under an injunction to keep him in his proper place, as he thought it folly to educate him above his station. But Henri has at different times rendered me great service, and observing that he possessed an intelligent mind, the tutors I placed over my own son have also had charge of him. His low parentage, and the manner in which his father parted with him, has been a source of continual mortification to him.'

'Poor fellow,' said Clifton, 'I pity him from my soul; but are you sure there was no villany in the affair? His pretended father might have stolen him from a respectable family, for it seems contrary to nature that a parent would turn away his own offspring in such a cruel manner.'

'It is possible, but if even so, I know of no way to discern the truth. My friend is dead, and Henri has no recollection of the home of his infancy.'

Clifton made no reply, but he thought he would write Mr. Hereford, and make some inquiries, which might, perhaps, lead to the truth. The captain soon after returned to his quarters, promising Ines to see her often, if her father permitted it.

Several weeks passed away. Stanley had recovered, and was at his usual station by the side of his captain. Alphonso, also, was now well, and preparing to go to Vera Cruz, and from there to the United States. Captain Clifton visited often at Senor De Montaldo's, who sometimes received him with all the cordiality of sincere friendship; at others he was grave, almost cold, while his appearance denoted the conflicts of his mind. He had grown pale and melancholy. His step was no longer elastic, but slow and wavering. Clifton had many times requested an interview, that he might formally declare his love for Ines, and request a favorable answer, but the subject was always evaded, and now he heard it whispered, that as soon as Alphonso left home, his father and sister were going to the city of Mexico: of course the motive was to remove her from him.

The day before his young friend was to leave, Clifton went as usual, to pass an hour with Ines, and imparting to her his firm conviction that her father would never consent to their marriage, he plead with all the earnestness of his deep affection, that she would consent to a clandestine union. She confessed that he possessed her whole heart—that a parting would make her very unhappy—yet she could not think of violating her promise to her father. She wept as she said this, but in a moment she rose, and giving him her hand she said, 'We will together go to him; perhaps he may relent.'

Before they reached the door, however, it opened, and Henri appearing, said, 'Senor De Montaldo would be glad to see Captain Clifton a few moments, in his library.' Leading Ines to a seat, he pressed her hand, and followed Henri from the room.

As he entered the room, Don Carlos was sitting with his face buried in his hands. Raising his head, he pointed to a chair, then as he saw Arthur about to address him, he exclaimed, 'I know what you would say; but oblige me by first listening to *me* for a few moments. I know, Senor, that you love my daughter—that you wish to make her your own. I know, also, that her heart is entirely yours; that to force her to marry another, would very soon give her a resting-place in the grave. And believe me, my friend, I think you worthy of her; and there is none on earth with whom I would sooner entrust my daughter's happiness than yourself. Being forced to act so different, from what an affectionate parent would wish, is the misery of my life.

'The father of Colonel Zenovia, though much older than myself, was my most intimate friend; and when my sweet Ines was an infant, we made a sportive engagement between her and *his son*. As years passed on, he was continually pressing me to promise him sincerely that our playful engagement should be considered binding. But I answered that 'I should never force my child to act contrary to her feelings; but still I would mention the young Zenovia as her future husband, and she might, perhaps, think of no other. As he grew older, however, I saw much in him to dislike, and determined unless she really loved him, that my sweet girl should never be his.

'About a year since, Senor Zenovia was taken very ill, and fearing he should die sent for me, and then asked me to promise that our children should be united as soon as Ines returned home. I refused, and after exhausting every argument, he suddenly told me he had the power to bring disgrace upon myself and family; to throw obloquy on the memory of my father, and the world should be apprised of what he knew, unless I promised to accede to his wishes.

'I indignantly repelled his accusation—told him he knew my father's life had been as free from fault, as any man in the republic—that he had multitudes of friends, and never an enemy. Zenovia requested me to ring a bell standing in the room, and said a few words to the servant who answered it, who immediately brought forward several letters, which he opened and made me read. It is useless to repeat what the letters contained, but they were apparently in my father's handwriting; and if known and believed, would, as he said, degrade my father's memory, and myself through him.

'I spent a few moments of agony, but at last told him he might do his worst; I believed the letters forgeries, and my child should be free; I walked to the door. At the moment I heard him tell his servant to go and bring a justice, and several witnesses, that he might give his deposition and make it public. The man was passing me at the door to go out. I stopped him. Disgrace to myself I could bear; but my father, than whom a better man never lived, I thought I had no right to allow such obloquy to be cast upon his memory; and in a broken voice I promised compliance with his wishes, if he would give the letters into my hands. This was done; and I vowed solemnly that my daughter should give her hand to his son.

'Then Zenovia assumed his usual friendly manner, said that nothing but the knowledge that his son would be unhappy if deprived of her he loved, had made him take his course; and that his friendship for me remained unchanged. I could not bear to listen to him, and hastened home, where I compared those letters with others I knew my father to have written, and was convinced to my great joy, by the writing and style, that they were base forgeries, though the hand was well counterfeited.

'Early the next morning, I rode to his house, eager to dissolve my promise and confront him with his villany; but judge my anguish when I found he was dead. Now there was no retracting; my oath could not be cancelled. I hurried home, and for weeks after was not able to leave my house. The most horrible suspicions have sometimes entered my mind in regard to my father's death. He was invited to dine at Don Jose Zenovia's with twenty other gentlemen; and from the moment in which he left his friends to return, I never was able to discover the least trace of him. It was believed that he was robbed and murdered on his way home. Several years after, a skeleton was found hidden away, and partly covered with rocks and earth, which Don Jose insisted was my father, and I had all due honors paid to the remains; but I never was satisfied; and since Zenovia's death, I have imagined he might have known more about that death than he chose to acknowledge.

'Thus you see, Senor, how I am placed. I have confided these circumstances to your honor, believing your heart will not condemn me as having done wrong.'

We will not repeat Clifton's arguments to prove that a vow made under such circumstances could not be binding; or how he plead that the happiness of his children should be of more consequence to him, than a promise so given. Don Carlos paused a moment, then said—

'I have told you before, that in my heart I would gladly receive you as my son, could it be so; but after what I have said, you cannot surely expect me to *see* you married, or that I should *consent* to its taking place.'

His strong emphasis on the word *consent*, and the piercing glance he bestowed upon our hero, made his heart beat strangely. He looked eagerly in the face of Montaldo, to see if there was anything there, to explain his equivocal words. But he turned away quickly, saying, 'You may tell Ines what I have related to you;' and Clifton bowing, left him.

As the door closed, the old gentleman said to himself—

'Will he take the hint? Surely if he regards his own happiness very much, he will understand and act according.'

As Clifton entered the room where Ines had remained, trembling with anxiety and suspense, he pressed her to his heart, while his eye sparkled with hope and expectation—

'Now my love,' he cried, 'you will not refuse to give me your hand? I will provide a priest, and to-morrow you will give me the right to protect you through every danger. Your father will soon forgive us, and then we shall have no more fear of Zenovia.'

Ines looked up at him in amazement!

'What can you mean?' she cried; 'have you lost your senses?'

'O no, I have just gained them.' And sitting by her side, he related the particulars of his interview, and ended, by saying he felt assured her father would be glad to know they were married, though of course he could never consent to it.

He spent a long time combating her objections, and at last drew from her a trembling consent.

'But not to-morrow,' she said, 'my dear brother goes to-morrow, and I should not be able to support additional agitation.'

Her lover endeavored to persuade her that it was wrong to delay their union, as something might happen to prevent it entirely; but she was firm, and he was obliged to acquiesce.

The very next day, Clifton gave Alphonso several letters, and begged him to deliver those to his mother and cousin himself; as he thought his friend would find a visit there pleasant, and *they* would be most happy to meet one who had seen *him* so lately.

Montaldo promised all he desired, and receiving the blessing and prayers of his parent and sister, he left them. Clifton engaged a Catholic priest (as there was none other to be had), and thinking there was nothing now to prevent the completion of his hopes, resigned himself to sweet dreams, in anticipation of the morrow. But alas! 'There's many a slip 'twixt the cup and lip;' and our hero found the adage verified in this instance. Before daylight, he was roused to take the command of one of the three detachments to be sent out to guard in a train, which was approaching from Vera Cruz, and which General Scott feared was not sufficiently guarded.

Captain Clifton had but an hour to prepare in, and the project of the day was not to be thought of. He wrote a few lines hastily to Ines, explaining how matters stood; and gently, *very gently*, chiding her for the delay which had prevented their union, and he left the city.

CHAPTER X.

*The mustering squadron, and the clattering car,
Went pouring forward with impetuous speed,
And swiftly forming in the ranks of war.*—BYRON.

It was scarcely later than sunrise, when Captain Clifton rode forth from the city, at the head of his company, with his lieutenant as usual by his side. The warm sun shone brightly upon their uniforms and glittering epaulettes; and they rode gaily along, chatting upon every subject which the lively fancy of the young soldiers suggested. Nothing of particular interest occurred, until towards evening, when they were descending a steep hill, where the road was overhung on one side by huge masses of rocks, with deep chasms yawning between, as though thrown into that form by some convulsion of nature. On the other side, a low chapparal at a little distance from the road communicated with a ledge of rocks extending into the country.

The advance had reached the bottom of the hill, and were crossing a little valley at its foot, when one shot and then another whistled through the rocks. The horse of the leader reared, and plunging, nearly threw his rider, so sudden was the movement. Wheeling around on the instant, he commanded a halt, and forming his men, dashed forward to the chapparal, from which the shots proceeded. They were met by a shower of balls, but nothing daunted pressed on.

At the same moment, Captain Clifton, who had commenced descending the hill, saw the movement and the occasion of it; and casting a piercing glance around, he discerned among the rocks on the opposite side, lances gleaming in the sun. Instantly comprehending their designs, he divided his men into two parties, and giving Stanley the command of one, ordered him to charge directly through the rocks; while he with the remainder dashed down the hill, and entered from below. Leaving their horses in charge of several of their number, the captain led his men on foot through the defiles.

Nearly a hundred men rose from their hiding places, as the small company appeared, and presented a formidable front of bristling lances. Clifton, after a first discharge of their pistols, gave the order to charge sword in hand. The guerrillas were too intent upon saving themselves, by placing the broken rocks between them and their foes, to strike very sure; and they were driven from rock to rock, leaving numbers stretched upon the earth, by the fatal weapons of our gallant company. At last, panic struck, they threw away their arms and sought safety in flight. At the same moment a number of flying lanceros came rushing down from above, closely pursued by Stanley, and his victorious soldiers. The remains of the party now disappeared; and the captain recalling his men, found they had lost six of their number, while many of the enemy had fallen to rise no more. They had scattered their foes like the wind, and not one was now visible.

Nothing farther obstructed their march, and soon after noon on the following day, they met the train they were to conduct onward in safety. The meeting of the two companies was cordial; and when they halted to take their evening meal, each party related the incidents of their march. Clifton met many acquaintances in the escort, and inquired about old friends whom they had seen more lately than himself. When passing through the rocky valley where they had been attacked coming out, they took every precaution to prevent surprise; but they were not molested, as the guerrillas probably found the rocks not as safe concealment as they fancied. When they were within ten miles of Jalapa, a large body of lanceros were discovered hovering near them. They were mostly on foot, only a few of the officers being mounted. They kept just out of pistol shot, but continued in the same direction for some time. The escort several times sent out parties to scatter them; but they would evade the attack, separate, and seem entirely dispersed; then in five minutes unite again, and go on as before. Suddenly they paused a moment, and then upon a signal from their chief, darted forward for the centre of the train, which they supposed to be of the most value.

Captain Clifton was stationed almost at the exact point where the attack was made. Calling upon his men to stand firm, they discharged a shower of balls upon the guerrillas, as they advanced upon them. Their onset was so fierce, that though many of their number fell, it did not stop their progress. On they came, with their long lances poised in their hands, giving many severe wounds. At the first assault, Clifton's horse was wounded. Maddened by the pain he became unmanageable; and rearing and plunging, he struck down several men who were aiming at his rider's life. Bearing him into the very centre of his foes, he received another wound, and fell. Disengaging himself from the saddle, Clifton sprang to the ground. He was alone and expected death; but resolved to sell his life as dearly as possible. His sword drew blood at every stroke, and many fell beneath his aim.

Enraged that one man should make such havoc among them, they hemmed him in close, and bleeding from a dozen wounds, it seemed that nothing could save him; but at this moment the Mexicans fell back on either side of him, and the faithful Stanley, at the head of his men, reached his captain's side. Throwing himself from his horse, he assisted Clifton to mount, and taking another himself, they spurred back to rejoin the escort. The guerrillas were now flying on every side; but they were not pursued far, as there was little fear of another attack. Cupidity had suggested the present one, and they fought with more courage than they would have done under some other circumstances. The commanders immediately ordered the wounded to be collected, and in a few hours they were in the city.

Clifton's wounds were not dangerous; as after having them dressed he rode into the town. As soon as he was able, and released from his engagements, he hastened to Senor De Montaldo's, and was very much surprised to find the house locked; and judging from the perfect silence reigning through it, uninhabited.

For a few moments our hero paused, undecided what to do; then recollecting that there was a cousin of the family residing in the city, after some hesitation, he decided to visit there, and if possible, find the reason for this singular movement. He was received coldly, and his inquiries answered evasively. Vexed at their suspicions, he assumed rather an air of hauteur, told them he was a friend of the family, and having been absent several days, he was surprised on his return to find they had departed. 'But it is of little consequence,' he said, turning away.

The gentleman now rose, exclaiming:

'May I ask your name, Senor?'

'Captain Clifton, of the United States army,' said our friend, haughtily. 'Perhaps you may have heard it.'

Arthur was passing out of the door, when the gentleman stepping forward, laid his hand on the other's arm, crying:

'I have indeed heard that name, and have every reason to respect it. Forgive me, Senor, for treating you so rudely. Just step back to a seat, and I will tell you all I know of my cousin. He supposed that as soon as the conquering army left the place, it would be left unprotected from the hordes of robbers that infest the country; and he could not think of exposing his lovely daughter to such danger. Therefore placing most of his valuables in security, he yesterday started with his family for the capital.'

'Did he leave no word with you for?—' Clifton stopped embarrassed.

'He did not; but he may have left some message with one of your officers. It would be singular if he has not.'

'Strange indeed,' muttered Clifton to himself. 'But are you sure,' he continued aloud, 'that they were provided with passports, and what was necessary to render their journey secure?'

'O yes,' replied the gentleman, 'he said he had everything prepared.'

Clifton thanked him for his information, and hurried to his quarters; where locking himself in his room, he remained several hours a prey to the most agonizing emotions. He felt really displeased with Ines, that she should have gone away so secretly, without leaving the least message for him. After what had passed, he looked upon her almost as much his wife as though the ceremony had been performed; and he thought she had treated him ill. That Senor De Montaldo should leave him, after their last conversation without any explanation, surprised him; but that Ines, whom he almost adored, and whom he thought the most perfect of women, should consent to such a measure, without expressing one word of regret for leaving him, when a few more hours might have united them forever, grieved him to the soul. Clifton was possessed of the most tender and delicate feelings; and though composed and dignified in his exterior, yet when he formed an attachment, he loved with his whole soul. No son, lover, or friend, could be more devoted than Arthur in all these relations; and though not jealous, he was quickly susceptible of any change or slight in his friends. Too proud, however, to allow such feelings to have long dominion over him, he roused himself to exertion, and although he could not banish regret, he very soon commenced as usual to hope for the best.

The army remained but a week longer in Jalapa, and then set out for Puebla. It is not our design to give a circumstantial account of the movements of the army, or the sanguinary battles in which they fought and conquered, but merely give a few incidents, occurring in their victorious march to the capital city of the republic.

They remained more than two months in Puebla, receiving supplies and new detachments of troops, and making occasional overtures of peace. The first week in August, the army again commenced their march. They met with many obstacles to impede their progress; but nothing could daunt the ardor of the brave troops, they still pressed on; and on the 18th of August reached the town of San Augustin, where a skirmish took place.

The next day at noon, commenced the battle of Contreros, and it was nobly sustained until dark. The firing on both sides was incessant; and to the Mexicans peculiarly fatal, till night and a heavy rain closed the scene, by separating the combatants. Very early the next morning, a portion of the troops in a gallant assault, led by Colonel Riley, turned the enemy's batteries, driving double their number from their guns, and taking several hundred prisoners.

As soon as the intelligence of this victory met General Scott, who was on his way to reinforce the attacking party, he sent General Worth (to whose brigade Captain Clifton was attached), to take possession of San Antonio, a village two miles distant. They attacked the enemy with such impetuosity, that although the Mexicans' grape and canister flew like hail through the ranks, and put many a brave fellow *hors du combat*, yet there was not the least sign of wavering. The officers evinced the most determined bravery, plunging into the thickest of the engagement; and there was no hesitation among their eager followers. The Mexicans were soon forced to evacuate the place, and were hotly pursued by the victors. As they neared the city, they made another desperate stand at Churubusco, which was strongly fortified; but though their resistance was obstinate, the impetuous valor of the United States troops, was not to be withstood. They carried the entrenchments, made many prisoners, and pursued the enemy to the very gates of the city. Our two *friends* had not been idle during the combat. The young captain led on his brave men with the steady courage of a veteran. Twice had he warded a deadly blow from the breast of Stanley, who eager only for victory, thought not of himself.

In the meantime, the commander-in-chief with another division, had taken the strongly entrenched position of San Pablo, after a fierce action of more than two hours; all of which time there was a continuous roar of cannon and musketry. The Mexicans, though having every advantage of position and weight of guns, could not maintain their ground against soldiers, every *one* of whom was determined to conquer or die; and the whole armament with a great number of prisoners were taken. Thus ended the day. *Four* distinct battles had been fought and won, the enemy numbering nearly four to one.

The next day the army marched to Tacubaya, within full view of the city of Mexico, where they halted, and received a flag from the city asking terms. Several flags were interchanged, and in two or three days an armistice was agreed upon, Scott dictating his own terms, and commissioners appointed to treat for peace. On the 8th of September the negotiations having closed with as little prospect of peace as ever, and the armistice being declared at an end, General Scott ordered an attack on Molino Del Rey, in which he was as usual victorious; though with the loss of many of his brave men. The next day, skirmishes were frequent. Captain Clifton was ordered out with his company to reconnoitre a certain point of the enemy's fortifications, and to report the probability of success, in an attack upon that position. Vaulting into the saddle, our hero felt scarcely himself, without the presence of his bosom *friend*, who, from a severe wound received the day before, was unable to accompany him. Suppressing a sigh, he rode onward. As he approached the works, in turning a height, they came suddenly in full range of the enemy's battery, which opened upon them, making sad havoc in their ranks. Retreating from this dangerous position, instantly but in perfect order, they the next moment encountered a large party of infantry, which very nearly surrounded them; but by his usual quick thought, the captain avoided that, and turning aside, they passed in safety through a route, cut up by ditches and rough broken ground.

Clifton, as he prepared to clear the last ditch, turned in his saddle, and sent a parting ball as evidence of his good will, when his horse stumbled, and tightening the rein to prevent his falling, he endeavored to spur him over; but instead the horse reared and fell back upon his rider. His men saw not the disaster, and in a moment a hundred Mexicans surrounded him. With a powerful effort, he raised his steed erect, and made a motion to ride through the party; but twenty instruments of death were pointed at his breast, and as many more dark, menacing faces lowered around him. Seeing the folly of resistance, and feeling the effects of his fall, he submitted to stern necessity; though not without being sorely mortified that *he* should fall into the hands of the enemy as a prisoner. He was led off and that evening taken into the city.

CHAPTER XI.

*'Hist! thou man of blood, the sighing breeze
May waft thy secrets to the light of day.'*

WHEN Ines de Montaldo received Clifton's letter, informing her of his forced departure, and expressing his regret that she had allowed anything to delay their union, which now he feared would be entirely prevented, she wept as she thought he might impute her unwillingness at that time to want of affection for him. Her father soon after entered the room unperceived, and seeing the open letter, reached forth his hand to take it. She attempted to draw it away, but he held it firm, and looking into her face, said, calmly:

'What does he write that you fear to have me look upon?'

The poor girl could not utter a word! She dreaded to have him know that she had contemplated such an act of disobedience, and burying her face in her hands, she awaited her father's first words.

Reading the short epistle through, he exclaimed somewhat sarcastically:

'Strange, that after having consented to break your father's promise in this way, you should, by some capricious fancy, postpone the mad project till it would be of no use. However, as you doubtless wish to be very dutiful, we will start in a few days for the capital, where you will be secure from such persecution.'

Ines started. 'Surely, my father,' she cried, 'you will not go till he returns.'

'Why not?' cried the old gentleman; 'delays are dangerous. Captain Clifton did not think of delay, when he saw you upon the point of being struck to the earth, or when your father or brother were in danger, though of course it was very wise in you to ask delay, when his happiness depended upon immediate action.'

Ines turned away in mortification. She knew not how to explain her father's singular humor, so different from his usual appearance. After a silence of a few moments, he sat down by her side, and told her gravely that she must prepare to leave in two days, as he should take his whole family to Mexico, knowing there would be little safety for them here, after the army left, which would be

She could not oppose him, and therefore said nothing; but her tearful eyes and pallid countenance betrayed her feelings. She wrote to Clifton, explaining, as far as she knew, her father's motive for this change of abode, and with her eyes raining down tears upon the paper, she entreated him not to think coldly of her for what she could not avoid. She regarded herself as much his wife in soul, as though the sacred vows had been pronounced, and could never break her vows to him by bestowing her hand upon another. Had Arthur received this letter, it would have saved him many miserable hours. Don Carlos, though he had determined never to break his promise by consenting to his daughter's marriage with Clifton, yet he felt it was a cruel vow, and in his heart he hoped his friend would persuade Ines to a private union, and was vexed that she should have prevented it by what he termed maiden coyness, and he resolved to leave the town immediately, we fear almost as much to punish her, as to gain a place of safety.

They had no difficulty in reaching their destination, and Don Carlos immediately took up his residence in his own house, which had been left for nearly a year in the care of servants. As Ines threw herself upon her bed, the first night, she thought how different were her feelings a week before. Then, happy in the society of him she loved, with the prospect of being united so that man could never separate them; now, she was alone, had been hurried away, as she supposed, to avoid him, and brought where she would of course be persecuted by the bane of her life, Zenovia. She not only disliked him for some traits in his character, but despised him for his cowardice. She had heard much from her brother, of his shrinking from any service where he would be exposed to danger, and of his cruel treatment of some soldiers who were under him.

Had she never seen Clifton, she would have disliked Zenovia, but now that he seemed destined to part her from him she loved, her soul rose in abhorrence against him, and she would sooner die than unite her fate with his. Her mind was very much depressed, as she thought her sudden journey might prevent her again meeting Arthur; at all events, it might be many months before he could reach the city, and the dreadful 14th of September, the day in which her father had said she must bind herself forever to one she hated—that day might come, and there be none to save. Disturbed by these thoughts, it was long before sleep visited her eyes, and then the most frightful dreams harassed her, and the morning sun was a relief.

As soon as Zenovia found that Don Carlos had returned to the city, he called upon them. Had Ines followed the dictates of her feelings, she would have received him with haughty coldness, but policy made her treat him with civility. She was obliged to see much of him, but his society was distasteful to her, and she avoided him as much as possible. He perceived it, and having heard from some of the servants of Clifton's visits, he soon after, in a conversation, mentioned him in such a manner that Ines feared his suspicions were roused, and she exerted herself to appear indifferent to the subject; but her increased color, and evident embarrassment, did not escape unobserved. As she left the room, his eyes followed her with a look of malicious meaning, and he said to himself:

'Then it is true, as I have suspected, and this is the reason why I am treated with such indifference; but have a care, my proud lady, I can hate as well as love. A moment's hesitation, when the time arrives, and I shall have other means of obtaining my wishes. Revenge shall be my study.'

Slow and weary the months crept on, and then the news arrived that the United States army had appeared, and obtained decisive victories over the Mexicans in several battles, and were now at the very gates of the capital. The armistice allowed a suspension of hostilities for a time, and then commenced a struggle for the city itself.

Just at evening, on the second day after the armistice was broken, Ines, restless and uneasy, unable to sit at home, requested her father to ride with her a short distance in the city, to see a poor woman who had been sick a long time, and to whom she had paid many visits, never forgetting to accompany kind words with something more substantial. The city was quiet: the noise and tumult of battle had ceased for the day. Senor De Montaldo and his daughter visited the poor old Roxa, as they called her, and were returning, when just as they passed nearly opposite the city prison, they paused to allow a small body of troops to pass them. They halted, and opening, discovered a prisoner in their midst. But O, what were the emotions of Ines, when she recognized in him the beloved of her soul.

He sat proudly erect upon his horse, with an expression of perfect composure, almost of haughtiness, upon his broad brow. He gazed fearlessly around, and though, at first, many were the jibes and insults cast at him, his dignified mien caused them to shrink within themselves. At the moment that Ines recognized him, forgetful of everything but her lover, and his danger, she bounded from the carriage, and stretching her arms towards him, shrieked his name in agony.

Clifton turned at the sound of that loved voice, and would have sprung forward to meet her, but the iron grasp of many soldiers held him back, and struggling in vain for freedom, he was hurried away. Ines fell fainting into her father's arms, who reached her just in time to prevent her falling to the ground, and placing her in the carriage, they drove rapidly towards home.

Colonel Zenovia had witnessed this scene, and he understood it all at once. Had Ines seen him then, she might indeed have shrunk affrighted from him. His eyes glared with the fearful light of a demon's, while his lips were compressed, and his hands clenched in his rage. He remained motionless for some moments, then starting, he muttered to himself:

'Poor fools! do they think they will triumph over me so easily? I will move the powers of heaven and hell, but I will foil them yet. She shall never be his, in life at least.'

He walked over to the prison, and saying a few words to the guards at the entrance, he passed in, and seeking the keeper, for two hours was engaged in close conversation with him. When he emerged from the prison, a smile of malicious triumph played over his lips, for he thought himself now secure of vengeance.

Donna Ines did not long remain insensible; the acuteness of her feelings soon roused her. Gazing wildly around, she cried, as she clasped her father's hand convulsively, 'Was that a dream, a fearful dream, or was it indeed reality?'

Her father's saddened countenance answered her question.

'O, he must not die! you will save him,' she cried, clasping his knees, and looking imploringly in his face.'

'Calm yourself, my child,' answered the old gentleman, 'he will not die. He is a prisoner of war, and will merely be detained till the present struggle is over, and then, if not liberated entirely, will be placed upon parole.'

'But, my dear sir, Zenovia saw him carried into the prison; he knows my regard for Arthur, and I fear will enter into some scheme to deprive him of life. I believe him capable of anything evil.'

'Impossible! my love; such conduct would be visited by the authorities with severe punishment. Clifton is my friend, and I will use my influence to secure his safety from all secret plotting.'

The night passed heavily away. Ines fancied herself struggling in the power of Zenovia, and that Clifton rushed to her rescue, but could not reach her. Then the scene changed, and Clifton lay under the uplifted dagger of his enemy, which had already drank his life blood, and he was rejoicing in the completion of his revenge. She rushed forward to die with him, and in her agony awoke. Relieved to find she had been dreaming, and still fearful that it might prove true, Ines the next morning called Henri to her presence.

She extended her hand as he advanced, exclaiming, 'Henri, have I not treated you as a brother? I certainly regard you as such.'

He bowed, and glanced upon her face to see what was coming next.

She paused a moment, then said, 'I wish you to do me a service, as a brother would do for a sister;' again, she paused.

'I hope you do not doubt my willingness to assist you, if in my power,' answered Henri; 'you have but to command, and I obey.'

'No, no! Henri, I do not wish to command. I merely beg a favor. You know that Mr. Clifton is a very dear friend of my father, and that we are under numerous obligations to him. He is now in prison, and on you alone I depend, to find some means of releasing him. That cruel Zenovia, I am convinced, will use every effort to injure him.'

'Anything that I can do for his release,' he answered, 'shall be done cheerfully. I think much of Captain Clifton. But tell me what you wish, my dear madam.'

'Thank you, Henri, you are always obliging. I wish you to watch the movements of Zenovia, keep constantly near him, and learn, if possible, his designs. Then, if you can do so, find in what part of the prison Mr. Clifton is placed, and in some way deliver a message to put him on his guard. Will you do this?'

'I will do all that is within my power,' replied Henri, 'and from the state of confusion here, by reason of the war going on outside, I may be able to do as you wish.'

He left her immediately, and proceeded to the prison. Mixing with the guards, he entered into conversation with them, and affecting contempt for their enemy, and rejoicing that Captain Clifton, whose name was so well known to the guerrillas from his puissant arm, was in a place where he would not trouble them again, he gained all the information he desired, of the place of our hero's confinement, and also of Zenovia's interview with the keeper. Moving carelessly away, he examined the barred windows, till sure he had found the one he wished.

During most of the day he watched the movements of Zenovia, followed him unseen from his house to the prison, and from there to a low hovel, in one of the narrow dark alleys of the city. Here, however, he remained but a moment, and then went home.

Convinced, by what he had observed, that Senor Zenovia meditated some foul play towards Clifton, Henri, after imparting what he had learned to Ines, again set out, intending to convey a few lines to Clifton, if that was possible, and concert some plan for his escape or concealment till he could leave the city, or his own army entered. Approaching the dark alley, which he had before seen Zenovia visit, he heard his voice speaking in low tones to a man by his side. Creeping cautiously, as near as possible, he stood concealed by an angle of a wall, and listened to their conversation. The companion of Zenovia was of gigantic stature, but Henri could not see his face.

'Colonel,' said he, addressing Zenovia, 'I wish this bad job was done. These Americans seem to have charmed lives. They have always fought our men one to five, ay, and beat them too.'

'Pedro,' said the other, darting at him a look of withering scorn, not unmingled with some surprise, 'do I understand you aright? Your words would seem to imply that these northern barbarians have charmed away your courage and senses too. Giant as you are, you have no reason to doubt your success in this enterprise against an unarmed man. He must certainly sleep to-morrow night.'

'But,' said the other, 'this Senor Clifton is not a small man, and I have heard many of our soldiers speak of his marvellous strength and activity, and should I miss the first blow, he might overpower me.'

The colonel, though almost bursting with rage, dared not give vent to his feelings, but endeavored to soothe and encourage the old man.

'You have always served me well,' he said, 'why should you now refuse me this last boon? Assist me in this, and the other affair I mentioned to you, and that will be all of the kind I will ever ask.'

'You say well, master, I have always served you faithfully, and have done many black deeds for your father and yourself, without asking why; but now I am getting old, and I have not a dollar to pay for masses for my poor soul.'

'Is it the lack of money, my good Pedro, that makes you raise so many objections? Put that hateful captain where he will trouble me no more, assist me to secure that proud girl, as I told you, and you shall have gold to your heart's content.'

As he spoke he drew a purse from his bosom, and presented it.

'Here, take this, as an earnest for the future. Of course you will put the old man to rest before you sleep. I shall depend upon you.'

Pedro dropped the purse at his master's feet, and exclaimed, 'Colonel Zenovia, take your gold, if it is mine only on that condition; for I can never harm a hair of his head. That good old don? O never! It is quite enough that he has been denied the light of day for fifteen long years, without now closing his life by violence.'

'Then he must starve,' said Zenovia, biting his lip till the red blood gushed, with suppressed rage at being thwarted in any of his plans; but determined to conquer his passion, he turned after a moment's pause to the old man, with the bland, persuasive manner he so well knew how to assume, and said:

'Listen to me a moment. You are aware that this braggart captain is an American, and our enemy. He has come here to assist in destroying our country, and to make us slaves. I feel it the duty of every Mexican, to take the life of any or all of them who fall in his way; besides, they are all heretics, and if they have the power, they will burn our churches, and kill our priests.'

'Enough, enough,' interrupted the old man; 'I will do what I can to exterminate these intruders. Give me directions, and I will go this moment, and despatch one of them.'

'Thank you, my good friend,' said the colonel, extending his hand; 'that is like yourself. I knew as soon as you reflected a moment, you would be willing to do what is right for me, and I will reward you bountifully. By the promise of a heavy bribe, I have prevailed upon the jailor to mix opium in his food to-morrow night, enough to place him in a sound sleep. Then he is to set the door ajar, and be waiting near till you despatch him, when he will assist in securing the body. Several of the bars will be sawed through, and the window left open, that it may be supposed he has escaped. Now you understand the arrangements, do not forget; to-morrow at midnight;' and they parted, that man of wickedness and his tool.

Soon after they disappeared, Henri stepped from his hiding place, saying to himself:

'Well, I have discovered your villany, and with good fortune will prevent its execution. Turning into a shop near by, he pencilled a few lines on a slip of paper, and walked to the prison.

CHAPTER XII.

'Through the broken portal, over weedy fragments,
Thalaba went his way. Cautious he trod, and felt
The dangerous ground before him with his bow.'

When Captain Clifton was brought into the city as a prisoner, he thought it was more than probable he should never leave it alive. He had heard that Colonel Zenovia was there, and he knew enough of him to suppose that he would leave no means untried to free himself from such a rival. When he entered the army, he took his life in his hand, and if he died, it would be gloriously; but to perish in a Mexican prison, unknown, uncared for, even his very captivity kept secret from his friends—the thought was indeed painful; not that he feared to *die*, but *such* a death was appalling. During his ride to the city, he distanced the rude familiarity of his guards, by his dignified manner. When he reached his prison he turned to take one last look at the light of day, before he was shut out from it entirely; and what were his emotions when he saw and heard her whose memory had so long dwelt in his heart; and when forced away, it seemed that this one glimpse of her continued interest in him made the darkness within still more dreary. He was placed in a room alone, the massive stone walls and heavy grated windows seemed to render all hope of escape impossible. But even could he effect that, how long could he expect to remain free, when every person he met must be an enemy? The sight of Ines, when she so unexpectedly appeared before him, dwelt upon his mind as a presage of good; and he slept as soundly on his pallet of straw, as he would on a bed of down.

The next morning, when his breakfast was brought in, he endeavored to commence some conversation with his surly keeper; but he only answered in monosyllables, and soon left him. Clifton had been accustomed to so much life and activity for many months past, that the gloom and silence of the prison depressed his spirits. At evening, when his jailor came in, he tried to gain some information about the state of things without the gates; but he maintained a sullen silence, only passing around the room and examining the windows, as if fearing he might escape. The windows were high and strongly grated.

As the night advanced, Arthur drew a stool under one of the windows, and stepping upon it, stood a long time gazing out upon the night. The moon shone brightly, and he thought he saw a man walking slowly under the windows, and looking up anxiously towards him. Having some curiosity to know the meaning of these movements, he pressed his forehead against the bars and watched. The man held something white in his hand, and several times made a motion to throw at the window. An idea darted through the brain of our hero, that it might be intended for him; and putting his hand through as far as possible, he saw what he was now certain was a letter, ascending towards him; but the aperture was so small that he could not catch it. Another trial, with the same success; and then the man after some delay, placed it in the crevice of a long pole and again elevated it; Clifton this time took it, and the man instantly disappeared.

Opening the paper, he read by moonlight the following lines:

'Do not eat the food given you to-morrow night; it will contain death. You will find several bars of your window broken, and at eleven to-morrow night, as the moon will then be nearly down, if you would escape certain death, open your window and come forth. Just under the wall you will find arms and a disguise. Go a few rods straight forward, and you will meet a friend, who will conduct you to a place of safety.'

There was no name to this note, but Clifton could not dismiss the sweet hope that the man was a messenger of Ines; and descending from his stool he retired to his rest. The next day passed without anything to beguile the tedious hours, but his own thoughts. He knew that the letter he had received might be a contrivance of Zenovia to decoy him into danger, rather than to save him from assassination; but he preferred at least dying in the open air, and determined to run the risk. He thought as in the song,

'I take thy word, for in a place
Less warranted than this or less secure
I cannot be, that I should fear to change it.'

At evening he was removed from his room for a short time. Soon after he was taken back, his evening meal was brought in. He regarded the man who brought it with abhorrence, as he thought he was then plotting against his life. Of course he ate nothing; but placed his food under the mattress to prevent suspicion. He immediately examined the grating of the windows, and found three or four sawed through; so that by a little exertion, he could loosen them from the wall.

He waited impatiently for the appointed time, which he could only know by the decline of the moon. One sound after another died away in the building, and all was still. At last he thought he would delay no longer. Gently removing the bars one by one, which he found more difficult than he at first imagined, he found the aperture sufficiently large to admit him. Listening some minutes, and hearing no movement in the building, he sprung upon the stool which he placed under the window, and with a violent effort, raised himself to the aperture. Here he paused a moment, and looked to discover if there were any spies; but no sound struck upon his ear, and he swung down the length of his arms, and then allowing himself to drop, reached the ground without injury, save a sound shaking in every limb. Moving swiftly along close to the wall, he very soon discovered the arms his unknown friend had mentioned. Throwing off his coat and plumed cap, he donned a Mexican coat and broad brimmed hat, and affixing a false moustache to his upper lip, he deposited a set of citizen's arms about his person, thinking this was enough to assure him of his unknown friend's faith. In a moment he was moving with the fleetness of a deer, in the direction mentioned in the note, and had reached the borders of an old park, through which his path led, when he heard suppressed voices, and saw two figures advancing.

One of them paused a moment, whispering 'hist! did you hear nothing?'

They both listened attentively, and glanced cautiously on every side; but all being quiet, they were convinced their fears were imaginary, and advancing, halted opposite the place where our hero was concealed, and within a few yards of him; where he could not only hear their conversation, but see their countenances. At the first sound of voices, he had carefully ensconced himself within the thick spreading branches of a shrub pine, of which there were many in that part of the park; and though impatient to leave this dangerous vicinity, he was of course obliged to remain quiet where he stood.

One of the men before him, although the weather was warm, was so muffled in a cloak, that but little of his face was visible; but our watcher could perceive that his eyes were piercing and restless in their expression, while an enormous black moustache curled on his lip. There was something in his appearance, impressing Clifton with the belief that they had met before.

His companion was a man of gigantic frame, apparently about fifty-five years of age. His hair of mingled black and gray, hung in tangled masses around his neck and face. His eyes, deep set in his head, overhung by long shaggy eyebrows, and a deep cut across his upper lip, gave him a sinister and forbidding aspect.

'Well, Pedro,' said the first mentioned person, resuming their discourse, 'as you have promised to assist me, I will now unfold my plan for seizing Ines. You know she is very generous, and will risk even great danger to assist those who have awakened her sympathy. Two weeks since, I called upon her, and asked if she would take a poor orphan girl into her service. I said that a young girl had applied to me to find her a home, and I had promised to see and interest a young lady in her favor, who I felt assured by her well known benevolence, would protect her, even if there should be no vacancy among the servants; 'and now my dear lady,' I said, 'will you ratify the encouragement, I have given in your name, and add another to your many acts of kindness.' She consented, and I accompanied Camelia over immediately. I have seen her several times since, and she says her lady is becoming very much attached to her.

'Upon my instigation, Camelia has told her mistress of an old woman who was very kind when she was in distress, and has asked her to visit the old woman, in company with herself, which she has promised to do. This evening I saw the girl, and engaged her to persuade Ines to go with her to-morrow afternoon. The old woman will detain her till you arrive with a carriage, and bring her to me. I shall have everything in readiness to leave the city immediately, as Santa Anna is going to leave with the remainder of his troops. Ines will never marry me willingly. I must even try force. I am determined not to be disappointed.'

'But, colonel,' said Pedro, 'by forcing the lady away in this manner, you will lose her fortune, and that is all you ever cared for.'

'That is true, at least of late, but I do not intend to lose the fortune. The moment we are married, I shall demand it in her own name. It was the mother's fortune, and was bestowed upon the daughter.'

'Are you sure, senor,' asked the old man, 'that the girl will do as she says? She may betray us to Don Carlos, and—'

'O, I have looked out for that,' said the colonel. 'The girl is in love with one of my officers, and I have promised him to her, on that condition. Now, old man, do not fail, and uncounted gold shall be yours. See,' he continued, pointing to the west, 'the moon has sunk below the horizon; the signal of the affair up yonder,' pointing to the prison. 'Now go, and be silent and sure.'

The old man moved stealthily away, and Zenovia, after watching him till he disappeared, turned and walked rapidly toward his own house. As soon as convinced they were out of hearing, our hero rose from his hiding-place, and moved forward into the open space. At the same moment, a figure stepped from the opposite side to meet him. Knowing he was discovered, Clifton drew a pistol, and determined to await his approach, whether friend or foe. At the moment he heard his own name pronounced in a low voice.

'Ah, Henri,' he exclaimed, 'is it you, this is indeed a fortunate meeting. Did you hear what those villains have been contriving about entrapping Donna Ines into their power?'

'Yes, I heard it all, and shall repeat it to Don Carlos. I presume he will take measures to secure the rascals; but we have no time to stay here; you will soon be missed, and a search instituted for you.'

The friends now moved rapidly on together, Henry detailing all that had passed since Ines saw him led into the prison. Clifton's heart beat proudly, as he learned that his lovely mistress was the moving principle of his rescue. After some moments' silence, Clifton said—

'Henri, you may tell Senor De Montaldo that if he will select a party of men for the purpose of securing Zenovia, I will myself join him. I think I can do it without fear of detection. He would scarcely know me himself in this disguise.'

'I think you would do very well for a guerrilla,' said Henri, smiling.

They now turned suddenly from the densely populated part of the town, and striking into a narrow alley, soon entered a space where the buildings were very few, and of the lowest order. He stopped here, and turning to his companion, said—

'Are you superstitious? I mean are you at all afraid of ghosts?'

Clifton smiled.

'Ah, you do not *believe* in ghosts, then,' said his friend. 'Well so much the better. *There*,' pointing a little distance before him, 'is a building that has been deserted by human inhabitants for many years. It is said to be haunted, from strange figures having been seen entering and leaving it at midnight. Groans have also been heard issuing from the ruined arches, and when it has been searched, not a being could be discovered. It is now rarely ever approached, and has fallen into ruins. As you do not fear the spirits who have taken up their abode there, you will find it a secure refuge, while you are obliged to remain in concealment.'

Looking cautiously around, he stooped down, and moving a large stone, which leaned against a dilapidated building, he brought forth a small basket and a dark lantern, which he handed to Clifton. A few steps farther on, from a similar concealment, he drew a glittering sword. Our hero seized it.

'Now,' he exclaimed, 'with a good sword in hand, I fear neither ghosts nor men.'

As they parted, Henri said—

'If you are determined to come forth and join in the night's enterprise, you had best stain your skin with this liquid,' handing him a phial; 'you will better escape suspicion; and now good night. I shall watch till I see you safe in yonder house.'

Pressing the hand of his friend, Clifton moved away, and in a few minutes was groping his way along a broken wall to the interior of the building. As soon as he thought he would not be observed from without, he opened the lantern. Looking around he saw the room he had entered was entirely without furniture, while several of the windows were broken, and a gust of wind rushed through, nearly extinguishing the light. Following an impulse of curiosity, Arthur traversed one room after another. The doors, many of them were entirely broken down, others hanging by one hinge, and those that retained their upright position from being so long unmoved, creaked painfully on their hinges. The walls were crumbling in pieces, and covered with a damp mould, rendering the air very disagreeable. Passing quickly through these, he paused nearly in the centre of the house, before a door which was locked; but the key still remaining in it he turned it and found himself at the top of a flight of stairs. The air that met him was cold and damp; and closing the door, he sat down upon a window seat and mused upon the fate which had condemned such a vast and splendid pile of buildings to desertion and decay. The broken casements swung back and forth with a harsh grating sound, while the night wind moaned ominously through the crevices, and around the angles of the building. If Clifton had been in the least superstitious, he would have imagined the gloom peopled with beings not of human mould. After sitting a few moments, he heard or thought he did, a low groan. Starting up he listened, but it was not repeated, and supposing it only fancy, he resumed his seat; but soon again a low moan met his ear. It seemed to come from below. He rose and immediately opened the door, which led to the apartments under the ruins, and convinced by a faint and distant murmur, that he was not the only occupant of the place. Snatching up his lamp, and placing the basket of provisions on his arm, he descended the stairs. They were long, and at the bottom he found a door locked and without a key. He made several ineffectual attempts to force it open, then turning, he retraced his steps, and hastily traversing one room after another, without finding what he wanted, he at last stumbled, and nearly fell over something on the floor. Stooping, to his great joy he found it was a flat bar of iron, which had been loosened from some part of the building. Seizing it eagerly, he returned to the door. With several powerful blows, he battered the lock, so that with a great exertion of strength the door fell in with a sudden crash; the hinges which were nearly rusted through giving way. Throwing down his bar of iron, he passed swiftly on to another door, where the key remained in the lock. Opening it he paused, for he heard a faint voice murmuring—

'God is merciful, and has softened his heart that I shall not perish.'

Clifton started, and shuddered with horror. Walking the extent of the room, he discovered a door made entirely of bars of iron. In the centre, was a small square aperture, sufficiently large to admit a man's arm.

'O,' cried a feeble voice within, in the Mexican language, 'then you have come to give me food, and I shall not starve.'

'Starving,' cried Arthur, 'O, this is horrible; but you shall not starve, I will feed you.'

'O, Pedro,' said the voice, 'do not delay, or I shall die before you reach me; the death agony seems even now at my vitals.'

'I am not Pedro,' answered Clifton, 'but I will give you food;' and taking a biscuit from the basket he had continued to hold on his arm, he reached it through the aperture. It was so dark within, that Clifton could not see the being he was trying to feed.

'Ah,' cried the poor man, 'I cannot reach it. I have not tasted food for three days, and am too weak to rise.'

'Do not despair, my poor friend; I will find means to get it to you.'

Dipping the biscuit in some water, he placed it upon the point of his sword, and reaching through, the perishing man seized and conveyed it to his lips.

'O, bless you, kind senor, whoever you are,' he cried in faltering accents; 'this will prolong my life.'

Arthur cautioned him not to eat too much at first, as it would injure rather than restore him; and then attempted to loosen the grates of his prison, but they resisted all his efforts.

In a short time the old man (for such he seemed to be), by a great effort raised upon his knees, and clinging to the bars, said very feebly—

'O, senor, let me have one look upon your kind face; you are not Zenovia, or one sent by him; bless you, O bless you;' and losing his hold, he fell back motionless.

Clifton called to him repeatedly, but he moved not, he had fainted from exhaustion. Almost wild with the fear that he would die before he could reach him, Arthur caught up his lamp, bounded from the place, and hastened to where he had left the iron bar. Seizing it eagerly, he returned, and finding the old man lying in the same state, he now used almost frantic efforts to break the door. At last, when he feared he must give up in despair, one of the grates loosened and fell to the ground.

'Thank Heaven!' was his joyful exclamation.

Another and yet another yielded to his powerful arm, till the aperture was large enough to admit him. Passing through it on the instant, he took the old man in his arms, and carried him to a mattress spread in one corner of the dungeon, and there kneeling by his side, bathed his face in the best he had, cold water, and poured a portion of it into his mouth. It was a long time before the poor man gave any signs of life, and then he did not seem to realize his situation. Murmured blessings were constantly on his lips; but farther than that he was not sensible.

CHAPTER XIII.

*'And thus the villain's treachery is unmasked,
And the bright sun shines on his damning deed.'*

The morning light found Clifton yet at his post, and the hour of noon showed him in the same position. The old man had several times roused himself sufficiently to take a little food, and his watcher had nursed him with the care of a son. He had himself eaten nothing since the morning before, but he felt not the need of food, and for worlds he would not have taken one morsel of what might save the life of the perishing creature before him.

Soon after noon, the old man awoke from a quiet sleep of several hours. He was no longer oppressed with a stupor; his senses were clear, though he was very weak.

Taking the hand of his young attendant, he kissed it repeatedly, and then raised it to heaven, while his lips murmured blessings on his head. Our hero again supplied him with food and water, and after he had finished, asked him gently why he was there, and what person could be guilty of such atrocity as to confine him in that fearful place.

'I have not yet strength to repeat the tale,' sighed the invalid; 'very soon I will tell you. But first, my dear senor, tell me how you came to wander to this place, in which for fifteen years I have never seen a human being save my jailors? You speak our language, but, I think, are not a Mexican. And tell me, is it true that this city is besieged by a foreign army, as I have been informed?'

'It is true! and I am one of that army; but do not fear me on that account. I will save you from this dungeon, and protect you with my life. I was taken prisoner in a skirmish, a few days since, but having escaped from my prison wandered here for safety; and I am truly thankful that my misfortunes have enabled me to save a fellow-creature from so cruel a death as that to which you were doomed.'

'The holy virgin will bless you, senor. But tell me more about yourself. I love to hear you speak, and it has been so long since I have looked upon a face but that of those merciless beings, who at last left me here to perish, that I cannot remove my dim eyes from your face.'

Arthur, to please the old man, related some incidents of his life, mentioned his coming into Mexico, gave a slight account of the success of their arms, and then touched upon his acquaintance with Senor de Montaldo and family, and the villany of Zenovia.

The old man listened attentively, and at the close raised his clasped hands to heaven, crying, ' O, Powers of Mercy, I thank thee. Thou hast sent this man to bring wickedness to light, to preserve the innocent, and punish the guilty, and to restore thy servant once more to the bosom of his family.'

Clifton looked at him eagerly.

' Who then are you ?' he said ; ' who are your family, and who has confined you so many years in this gloomy place ?'

The old man desired to be raised, that he might sit up on his bed. He appeared to be very old. His hair, white as the driven snow, hung upon his shoulders ; his beard, of the same color, flowed down upon his breast. His face was colorless, and he was thin to emaciation. Clifton raised and supported him on his breast.

Turning his eyes upon Clifton, he said, ' My family was one of the first in Mexico, possessing wealth and influence. I have held many public offices, and have ranked high in the nation. I had many friends and but few enemies. I had an angel wife, who died a few years after our marriage, leaving me with one only child, a son, and he was all that a parent could wish. He loved me with ardent devotion, and when he brought one to his home, lovely, accomplished, and every way worthy of him, though he idolized her, there was no diminution in his reverence for me. I had a friend, at least one who called himself such, but we were opposed in politics. Many times we were opposing candidates for office, and as fortune would have it, I was usually elected against him. I knew it not then, but it seems that this embittered his mind against me, and though still openly professing the warmest friendship, he in secret meditated revenge.

' About fifteen years since we were placed again in opposition. For some time the contest was doubtful, but at last it seemed inclining in my favor. At this time I was invited, with some twenty gentlemen, to dine at his house. The time passed as usual on such occasions. Mirth and hilarity reigned ; gay conversation, in which all mention of politics was avoided, occupied the evening. It was late before the party separated, and my friend detained me a few moments, to listen to some new project he had just started, and then, mounting my horse, I rode slowly towards home. I had proceeded but a little distance, when a gigantic man started up before me, and giving my horse a severe blow, he started aside so suddenly, that carelessly as I was sitting, I was thrown to the ground. An iron grasp was placed upon my shoulder, a cloak thrown over my head, and I was dragged swiftly away. I struggled to free myself, to cry for help, but the fall from my horse had bruised me, and my mouth was so closely covered, that I could not make an audible sound. My captor paused several times, as if to take breath, and then pursued his course. I was very soon brought into a house, as I knew by the change of air, and the echo of his footsteps.

' I was dragged down a flight of steps, through several doors, which were locked after us, and then into this room. I was placed upon a mattress, and then I knew, by retreating footsteps, that I was about to be left alone. From being dragged along over a rough road, in such a harsh manner, my limbs were so bruised and sore, that it was with the greatest difficulty I could move. After several painful efforts I succeeded in removing the muffling from my head, and rose upon my hands and knees. I was in complete darkness. I called aloud, I shouted, I begged to at least be allowed a light, that I might view my prison—but echo only answered. The floor was of stone, and the walls of the same material. This, and the damp, cold air I breathed, convinced me that I was under ground, probably in a dungeon, from which I should never be allowed to move. I am not naturally fearful, but then an irresistible horror took possession of my faculties, and falling upon my face, I remained in a state between stupor and faintness, how long I know not, but probably several hours.

'When I came to myself, I was lying in the same position, but light shone around me, and I heard whispered voices near. I made an attempt to turn, but my limbs were so stiff and swollen, and pained me so cruelly, that I could not stir. Some one now approached, and rough hands raised me up, placing me on the mattress. The pain was so excruciating, that I groaned in agony. Raising my eyes I saw the same giant form bending over me which I had seen once before, and at a little distance, he who had pretended such devoted friendship for me, stood gazing with a cold, indifferent look, upon one whom he had so villanously entrapped.

'Turning my eyes full upon his face, with the powerful emotions of my soul speaking from them, he turned pale, and quailed beneath the glance. Turning away, he addressed a few words to his servant, and walked towards the door. Then all my indignation against my false friend gave way to the horrible idea of being shut up in darkness, denied the blessed light of heaven, and separated from my family and friends. In vain I begged him to stay and answer my questions; he turned away, with a sneering reply, that important business demanded his attention. Then all my indignation burst forth. I denounced the vengeance of Heaven upon his wicked head, told him he would never be happy, that the memory of this deed would haunt him while he lived, and render his death bed one of horror insupportable.

'He dashed out of the room, and, muttering curses, disappeared. I fell back upon the bed completely exhausted. Excitement had lent me temporary strength, but that was over, and I now lay, quite unable to move, while my attendant bathed my limbs, and, binding them up, presented me some food; but I could not eat, and putting it aside, requested, in as calm a tone as I could assume, to know the reason of this outrage. Pedro, for that was his name, said I was placed here by the order of Don Jose Zenovia, in revenge, because I had so long thwarted his wishes, and mortified his pride, and now, on my removal, he expected to gain his election, which would otherwise fall upon myself.

'But surely,' I cried, ' he does not think to keep me here unknown to all my friends. My son, I know, will ferret out his villany, and I shall not long remain here.'

'The man shook his head at this remark.

'" Alas, senor," he said, " I fear you will be disappointed. This old edifice belongs to the Zenovia estate, and for many years has been totally deserted, and even bears the name of being haunted. No one thinks of coming here, and Zenovia has taken his measures so effectually, that there can be no discovery, or even suspicion to fall upon him. It will be supposed that you have been robbed and murdered." After a pause of a moment, he added:

'" Senor Zenovia intends to confine you here through life. You will have food and lights brought you, and will be obliged to content yourself with your fate." He soon after left me, and for three days I did not see him again. For a short time I was supported by indignation, but it did not last long;

my spirits would not keep up under such dreary solitude, and the knowledge that it was to be forever.

'When Pedro came again, I was humble as a child, and besought him to tell Zenovia, that if he would free me, restore me again to life and liberty, I would swear solemnly never to disclose what had passed, but to find some excuse for my absence, which should not in the least affect him, as not wishing longer to engage in active life. I scarcely knew how high my hopes were raised until Pedro came again and they were blasted by disappointment. He said his master had considered a long time upon my proposition, but at last said he would do nothing about it—my fate was sealed, and I had better become reconciled to what could not be avoided. I will not weary you, senor, by particulars of my sad imprisonment.

'It was nearly two years before I saw Zenovia again, but he was then, as before, deaf to all my entreaties for liberty. He told me that a few weeks before a body had been found concealed, not far from where I was kidnapped, and my son had ordered all due honors paid to the corpse, supposing it to be myself—that time had already blunted the edge of his grief, and he was beginning to mix again with the world. He said too (which stung me more than all the rest), that my son had affianced his only daughter, the namesake and living image of my sainted wife, to his son.

'Fifteen years have passed away, and in that time I trust that I have become resigned to my fate, believing that when this mortal body should resign its breath, my Father would take me to be with him in paradise. Pedro furnished me with books to beguile the weary hours, and also writing materials, that I could transfer my thoughts to paper. This was entirely from a feeling of sympathy, as Zenovia would never allow me that small consolation. The perusal of those books has enabled me to live on and endure, and has directed me to the God of mercy for comfort in distress.

'For two years past my food has been brought to me by Pedro and the young Zenovia, alternately, my treacherous friend being dead. Four nights since, Zenovia came to me, and said the North American army were at the gates of the city, and might very soon enter it. If they did he could stay no longer here, and of course could not attend to my wants. He left me food and light for one day, and a dagger, saying when I felt tired of life, I was at liberty to use that.

'Ah, my friend, what thoughts of horror took possession of my soul, when after so many years confinement I was at last left to starve, or end my life by suicide. So you found me, and blessings the most precious will rest upon you, for your great kindness. You have mentioned Don Carlos de Montaldo—you must have conjectured, from my narration, that I am the father he has so long mourned.'

'Ah yes,' cried Clifton, whose emotion had been almost overpowering as he listened; 'ah yes! and it will be the happiest day of my life, when I can restore to him one so revered, and place you, my dear sir, in a situation of comfort and happiness.'

Arthur then unfolded to Don Juan the project of the night, and asked if he would be willing to remain there till the next morning, when he would return with means to convey him away in safety.

'Do not hesitate a moment for me,' cried the old gentleman; 'hasten, and secure the villains, then return for me. I am not strong enough to be moved to-night, and am so accustomed to solitude that I shall not fear to be alone.'

Clifton asked if he had writing materials still left, and being directed to them, he sat down and wrote a brief account of the state of the invalid, and where to find him, then directed it to Don Carlos, and placed it in his bosom. It was now growing towards night, as he found by going above, for it was all night below, and he commenced his preparations for going back into the city again. Staining his skin a tawny hue, and again affixing his black moustache, he arranged his clothes so that Don Juan said he would never be recognized.

The old man's courage faltered when he saw his preserver about to leave him, but yet would not consent to detain him a moment. 'I have perfect confidence in you,' he cried, and again our hero received his fervent blessings. He left the door open, and the remains of the food and water by his side, and also his lamp, which he supposed would last till morning, and then departed.

CHAPTER XIV.

*'Now seize the wretch, and bear him hence;
Let justice do her work upon the caitiff.'*

When Henri Duvalle returned home, he found all the family had retired to rest. Passing through a long corridor, on his way to his own sleeping apartment, he heard a door softly open, and looking round he saw Ines step into the passage.

'Henri,' she said, in a low, soft voice, scarcely above a whisper. He turned back instantly, and in answer to her inquiries, repeated what he had done for and with Clifton.

'Are you sure he will be safe there?' she asked eagerly; 'there are strange stories told about that old ruin: and did you not know it was on Zenovia's estate.'

'Yes, madam, but the senor has too much on his hands at present to think of pursuing Captain Clifton, if he even discovers that he has escaped. He has a new project in his head, which will be explained to you to-morrow.' He bowed, and the lady disappeared into her room.

The next morning, Don Carlos was informed of all that Henri had overheard, and of Clifton's intended visit that evening. Don Carlos listened to this account with the strongest indignation. He sent for his daughter at once, and when she entered, asked some indifferent question about her new maid, and then inquired if she had made a request that her mistress would accompany her to see an old friend.

'She has mentioned it several times,' replied Ines, 'and this morning, I promised to accompany her at evening.'

'Yes, perfectly right, my love,' now if you please, go and find out the precise spot where the old woman's house stands, and then come and tell me; but excite no suspicions of your object. Speak to her carelessly, as about an indifferent subject.'

'But may I not know my father?'

'Not at present,' he interrupted; 'after your return I will explain.'

She left the room, and Don Carlos selected the required number of servants, furnished them with arms, and obtained a promise of perfect secrecy and obedience from them. Ines found and gave her father the description he wished, and in return he explained his motives for the inquiry. Ines shuddered at the danger she was so near falling into, and turned to Henri with a bright look of gratitude.

He bowed, and smiled sadly.

Running up to him, she took his hand, and said in a soft, coaxing voice, 'Now, my brother, do not always look so sad, and throw a look of humility into your brow.'

'Have I not reason?' said Henri; 'of what should I be proud?'

'Well, I do not ask you to be proud of your sister, but still I claim that name, and my father loves you as a son. Do you not, my dear sir?' and she turned an appealing look upon him.

He smiled, and kissing her, said, 'Yes, my dear, Henri merits our warmest regard, and he certainly has it.'

Ines now tripped up to her chamber. A thousand ideas flitted through her mind. She felt a heavy weight removed from her heart, for she believed all fear of Zenovia was at an end. Coward as he was, she could not think he would dare approach them again, when his treachery was unmasked; and visions of hope and happiness filled her brain, in which the presence of our hero was indispensable to complete the charm. It was towards evening. Ines was sitting at her window, listening to the cannonading, which, during the day, had been still advancing nearer to the city, and noting an occasional shell as it entered, struck, and exploded. Messengers rode hastily to different parts of the city, giving accounts of the taking one position after another by the besieging army, and it was the general opinion that it could not hold out another day. It was also whispered that Santa Anna intended deserting the place, with a large body of chosen troops, leaving them to the mercy of the enemy, and alarm and confusion reigned throughout. Senor De Montaldo's house stood outside of the centre, and far removed from the scenes of commotion going on without, so that they seemed to enjoy comparative peace. As Ines looked, she saw a man coming up the street; he paused several times, probably to listen to the roar of ordnance. Just opposite her window he stopped, and seemed making some inquiry of a person he met. Why did her heart beat faster as she gazed on him? She could not tell! He was dressed as a common Mexican; his low top, broad brimmed hat, was drawn over his face, which was quite dark, and his upper lip was graced with a jetty ornament, customary with those of her country. But there was something in his movement, his graceful bow, as he left the man he was speaking with, and his quick glance upward to her window, as he rapidly crossed the street, and stood awaiting admittance at her father's door, that sent a thrill through her whole frame. Clasping her hands tightly over her heart, she sat tremblingly awaiting what would follow. But when half an hour passed, and everything was quiet as usual about the house, she said to herself, while a burning blush mantled her cheek, 'What a silly being I am, looking for wonders in every slight event. I ought to know that it would risk *his* life to come here. O, God grant,' she added energetically, 'that he will not venture out where I fear destruction will await him.'

At this moment a light step approached, and some one tapped at the door. She flew to open it, and Henri told her in a low voice her father desired to see her in the library. She followed him with tottering steps, several times opening her lips to ask him a question, and as often closing them with a sigh.

Henri left her at the door, and she entered alone. As she had imagined the stranger was there, in close conversation with her father. Don Carlos started up as he saw her, and saying, 'I can give you but a short half hour, disappeared from the room. Ines in amazement was just turning to follow, when a low voice pronounced her name, and Clifton, casting his hat to the floor, and taking the moustache from his lip, advanced and clasped her in his arms. 'Loveliest and best,' he cried, 'do I indeed once more hold you to my heart, and all my own? No fear now of a parent's frown on our love; with his entire approbation we must be happy.'

Ines hid her face a few moments on his shoulder, then raised her eyes and surveyed his countenance.

'Does my dark skin terrify you?' he asked with a smile. 'I think I may pass very well in the character I have assumed, since even you did not at first recognize me.'

Ines disengaging herself from his embrace, and moving to a seat, began to question him anxiously about the danger he ran in thus exposing himself. He soon quieted her apprehensions, and then they conversed of the future, which, to their vivid imagination, was just opening for them in perfect happiness.

But they were not long allowed this pleasure. Don Carlos entered: 'Come, Senor Clifton,' he cried, 'Henri has already departed with our small force, and we had better soon follow; but first we will secure that faithless girl, who so nearly drew my Ines into such peril.'

Arthur started up, and resuming his disguise, said to Ines, 'Dear lady, if you have any compassion, you will give me something to eat before I go, for I assure you I am quite ravenous.'

She bounded off at this request, and our friends took measures to prevent any trouble from Camelia, by placing her in a private room, under guard. When they returned, Ines had prepared a light meal with her own hands, not wishing to attract attention by calling upon the servants. Clifton really stood in need of food, having so long fasted, and thanking her more by his eyes than words, they immediately departed. Ines watched them with tearful eyes, till they disappeared in the distance, and then went to her room to pray for their safety.

Don Carlos and his friend walked on to the rendezvous, the former explaining as they went, the plan of operation. As they came near the house described to them, they parted, and each secured a position where they could command a view of the door. It might, perhaps, have been an hour, though to Clifton it seemed an age, and it was getting so dark that he could not distinguish objects plainly, the moon being hid by heavy clouds, when the roll of carriage wheels fell upon his ear. The sound approached nearer, and paused within a few rods of him. The next moment a figure descended the steps, and speaking a few words in a low tone to the driver, he peered cautiously around for a minute, and then walked swiftly towards the house. It was too dark to discern features, but from the enormous size of the man, Clifton judged it must be him they sought. Joining Don Carlos, they summoned two of the party concealed near, and together advanced to the door. Placing his ear to the door, Clifton heard a man's voice say, 'But what shall I do, old woman? Senor Zenovia will be furious, when I meet him alone. Is there no possibility of their coming yet?'

'O, no!' answered the old woman, 'Donna Ines would not come out so late. I am afraid they have discovered something about it, and so have kept her at home.'

At this moment making a sign for the others to follow, Clifton gently raised the latch and entered. 'Secure that woman,' he said, in an authoritive voice, to the two men. She was a very large person, and exerted her strength to the utmost, but at last with great difficulty she was secured, and a muffling placed over her mouth.

At the first glimpse of his enemies, Pedro endeavored to rush past them and escape at the door, but failing in that, he drew a pistol, and warned them to keep their distance. Clifton, with one bound, was at his side, and dashing up the weapon, it went off, but without injuring any one. Throwing it from him, a dagger instantly supplied its place.

By a sudden motion Clifton caught the ruffian's arms, and endeavored to pin them to his side; but he was powerful, and wrenching away, he inflicted a wound in Clifton's shoulder. Moving a step backward and drawing his sword, he said, gravely, 'Pedro, you fight well in a bad cause. We have no desire to injure you; it is your master we seek. You must see that resistance is useless,' pointing to his companions. 'You cannot escape us; give up at once, and life will be granted you, on condition of guiding us to Zenovia; but otherwise we shall be obliged to use unpleasant means to effect our purpose.'

The old man looked keenly at the speaker for a moment, then suddenly drawing another pistol from his bosom, he cried, 'I have no faith in your promises;' and pointing at his antagonist, the ball missed Clifton, and passing through the garments of Montaldo, slightly grazed his shoulder, and entered the wall beyond. Our hero saw where the shaft sped, and rushed forward, the whole determination of his soul darting from his eye. Pedro started aside, not however without receiving a severe wound. Darting forward within the sweep of the sword, he caught Clifton in his muscular arms, and endeavored to crush him with his great strength; but he found he had not a child to deal with. After a violent effort, Arthur succeeded in mastering his hands, and with almost superhuman strength, dashed him against the wall. Panting for breath, the giant stood erect a moment, then passing his hand upon his brow, he staggered forward and fell upon the point of Clifton's sword, and sunk to the ground. What we have attempted to describe, had scarcely been the work of a minute. The two men had just secured the old dame, and turned to assist Clifton as Pedro fell. Cords were passed around his limbs, and the blood staunched, which flowed freely from the wound in the breast. He made no resistance after he fell, but to all their questions he maintained a sullen silence. Clifton and Don Carlos consulted a few moments together, and then giving some orders to the two men with them, they disappeared at a back door.

Looking around, Don Carlos found a large cloak hanging near the door, and throwing it over Pedro, he with Arthur raised him on their arms, and bore him slowly towards the carriage. The night was so dark that the driver could only distinguish several figures moving towards him. Straining his eyes through the gloom, he said, 'Pedro, are you there?' Clifton assisted Don Carlos into the carriage with the wounded man, and then moving towards the speaker, said in a gruff voice, in imitation of the old man, 'All right; I have them safely caged, but I had to fight for it. Did you not hear the report of the pistol? It frightened her a little, I imagine. As soon as I get into the carriage, drive on with as little noise as possible, to the place where the colonel is to meet us.'

'I will,' answered the man. 'The colonel will think we have done a good night's work, and now on for our reward.'

The carriage now moved slowly forward. The road seemed endless, and Clifton was beginning to think the driver suspected him, and was taking them in quite a different direction from the first order. At last they stopped, and a voice outside asked, 'What success?'

'Excellent,' was the driver's answer, 'they're all here.'

'Then I will bring the colonel,' said the first voice.

'Now is my time,' whispered Clifton. 'You, senor, had better remain here and watch this rascal, while I join our little party, which I am sure must be very near us.'

He opened the door gently and stepped out. The moon shed a dim and uncertain light upon the scene; he saw that they had left the buildings behind them, and he judged from appearances, that they must be on the outer confines of the city. A few broken ruins of what had once been the walls of a house, rose upon the eye, dark and ragged in its outlines, and an occasional tree cast a shade over the ground. His eyes roamed anxiously in search of his men, but he could see nothing. His ear, however, took a slight sound of murmuring voices, in the direction of the ruined wall. Advancing cautiously, he muttered one word in a voice so low that only a careful listener could have heard it; but it was answered in the same tone, and he knew his small but resolute band were there.

At the same moment he saw several figures advancing towards the carriage. Giving the word to his eager followers, they moved stealthily along in the same direction. Not expecting an assault, they started back in surprise, as the little party rushed upon them, sword in hand. Zenovia, who was in front, made a bound to reach the carriage, but the muzzle of a pistol met his breast, and he threw himself back into the midst of his men. The moon now streamed forth with its full lustre, revealing each party to the other. Stepping a little in advance, Clifton said, 'Mexicans, soldiers, we come to arrest a criminal; we seek your chief; leave him in our hands, and you can depart in peace; resist, and you force us to take him by violence!'

The men looked at each other in silence. Zenovia, fearing that they would indeed leave him, glanced upon them to discover their feelings; waving his sword he exclaimed, 'Forward, men! Who talks of deserting his chief? On, I say, they are but a handful!'

Thus encouraged, the attack which now commenced was repelled with firmness for a few moments. Zenovia, while surrounded by his men, felt very brave; but when he saw them falling about him, a deadly panic seized him, and he turned to flee. Clifton's eye had never left him for a moment, and as he noted this motion, he told Henri, who stood by his side, to take those who remained, prisoners, if possible; but not allow them to escape, as they could easily bring an overwhelming force upon them. Then with the speed of the wind, he followed Zenovia. The latter turned, and seeing but one person near, for one moment actually thought of turning upon his opponent, but his innate want of courage forced him onward. Fear instead of giving him speed retarded his flight, and Arthur immediately overtook him. Forced to extremity, Zenovia now turned and attempted a desperate thrust at our hero's breast. Parrying it with another, he knocked the sword from his hand, and with the strength of a single arm stretched him upon the ground.

'I ask my life. O, have mercy!' cried the terrified wretch, raising his hands.

Clifton looked at him with an expression of such scorn, that the coward shrank away to avoid a second. At this moment Henri approached.

'Captain,' he said, 'everything is accomplished. We have taken five prisoners—the rest lie where they will never move again.'

'Then we will return immediately,' replied Clifton.

They bound Zenovia's hands, and secured his mouth. By the young captain's order, the wounded prisoners were placed in the carriage, with two of Don Carlos's party, who were severely wounded; the rest were compelled to walk; and they moved silently, but swiftly as possible, towards home.

It was after midnight when they halted at Senor de Montaldo's door. The prisoners were placed in separate rooms, with a guard over them. Don Carlos's family physician was called in, and the circumstances being explained to him, he immediately dressed their wounds, and they were left to repose.

Early the next morning the United States army marched into the city. As soon as it was consistent, Captain Clifton repaired to meet the commander-in-chief. He was received by his brother officers with cordiality; and his own particular company welcomed his re-appearance with shouts of joy. But Stanley—who can describe his transports, when he once more pressed to his breast the friend he loved as his own life, and of whom he had not been able to obtain the slightest trace since his disappearance. Clifton requested permission to take a portion of his company, that he might guard from danger those friends who had saved his life; as in the present state of the town there was much to be apprehended from the uprising of the people. In consideration of his services, this was granted. He left twenty of his men at Senor de Montaldo's, charging them to keep strict watch over Zenovia, to whom he now revealed himself. Zenovia grew black from rage and mortification, when he found that he had been foiled at every point by his rival, and turning away, deigned no reply. Arthur remained but a few moments, and then departed with the rest of his company for the ruins.

Meanwhile, Senor de Montaldo was sitting by the side of the dying Pedro. The surgeon had told him he could not survive the day, and Don Carlos was urging him to confess what he knew of his father's fate. He had heard Henri's account of the conversation between Zenovia and his servant, and suspicions before aroused, now become agonizing. He begged Pedro to relieve his anxiety, and tell him if his father had indeed been murdered. He promised that he should be released and enabled to leave the country, if he would but tell the truth. For a long time Pedro continued a sullen silence; at last he turned to Montaldo—

'Will you promise, senor,' he said, 'that, should I recover, I shall not die for my crimes? I am too wicked to die. I would live to repent and make some reparation.'

'I promise you, solemnly, that it shall be as you wish.'

'Senor,' resumed Pedro, 'commanded by my superior, I have injured you greatly.—Your father has lived in close confinement fifteen years. Don Jose Zenovia commanded that he should have no comforts, but merely food, to sustain life. He hated the old don, because he was his rival, and so put him out of the way. But, senor, your father will tell you that I provided him with many comforts which were forbidden, by both father and son.'

He then started, as if a sudden and painful recollection crossed his mind. He covered his face with his hands, and exclaimed;

'O, senor, why did you wish to know all this? Why, did I ever tell you, now that it is too late?'

Senor de Montaldo had listened with agonizing emotion to the old man's words.

'What do you mean? Why too late?' he cried; 'surely, you will tell me where he is?' and he clasped the hard hand of the other in both his, while his eyes were fixed with imploring eagerness upon his face. The old man sobbed:

'Alas! it is four days, since he has had food. The cruel Zenovia wished me to take his life; and when I refused, he said he must starve, as he was going to leave the city, and could have no more trouble with him; and, blessed Mary forgive me, I obeyed, and have not seen him since.'

Don Carlos sprang to his feet—his eyes glared furiously upon the man before him. He seized his hand with a gripe that made him cry out with pain.

'Tell me,' he cried, 'tell me quick where you have put him. Tell me, I say, or I will—'

His head drooped upon his breast.

'O!' he added, in a tone of the most exquisite misery: 'surely, my heart will break with this agony.'

At this moment the door opened, and Clifton entered.

'My friend,' he said, approaching Don Carlos, 'prepare your mind for a surprise; a happy one, I think.'

'Happy!' ejaculated he. 'O, Clifton—he—my father—O, horror!'

Arthur understood at once what he had been listening to, and hastened to undeceive him. Opening the door by which he had just entered, he was immediately followed into the room by several men, bearing on a mattress a pale and emaciated form. They laid it down at Clifton's feet, who, raising the aged man tenderly in his arms, placed him upon a couch. Then taking his friend's hand, he led him forward.

'He is not dead, my dear sir,' he exclaimed. 'God in his mercy has preserved and restored him to your affection.'

Don Juan raised himself upon his couch and extended his arms, while his son clasped him again and again to his heart. They were both overcome with emotion; and Clifton motioned his men to leave the room, while he himself retreated to the bed-side of Pedro, who was groaning inwardly.

'Now I shall die more happy,' he murmured, faintly. After a pause, he continued:

'There is another thing I wish to confess, before I leave the world.'

'Confession and repentance,' said Clifton, turning to him, 'will even at the eleventh hour obtain pardon.'

'I hope so,' was the poor man's ejaculation. 'Where is Henri?' turning his dim eyes about the room. 'I have something to say that will remove from him the imputation of disgrace, and I hope will enable him to return to home and family.'

Clifton started.

'Then there was villany in the manner of his removal from France? Do not delay to make the confession, and very much good may arise from it.'

At this moment Don Juan called Clifton to his side. Placing his hand in that of his son, he said:

'Carlos, to this kind being I am indebted for life—for preservation from the cruel death of starvation. O, cherish him in your heart's care; he is worthy of far more than you can bestow.'

'He has ever been the preserver of me and mine,' cried Don Carlos; 'from the first day he ever saw one of my family, he has not ceased to confer benefits upon us.'

He paused a moment, then turning to Ines, who had entered the room unperceived, he placed her hand in that of our hero.

'Take her,' he exclaimed; 'she is yours, with the free and full consent of her father; and believe me, I have suffered much, when forced to treat you with coldness, for even one moment.'

Arthur encircled Ines's waist with his arm, and both kneeling at Don Carlos's feet, besought his paternal blessing. He gave it with tears, and eyes raised to heaven.

'Ah!' cried the happy lover, 'this one moment is full compensation for all my sufferings, since it assures me that our love is fully sanctioned.'

Rising, he led his affianced bride to Don Juan.

'My love,' he said, 'look upon your revered grandfather, who for fifteen years has been closely confined under the orders of the Senor Zenovia, and tell me if we have not reason to be thankful, that we have escaped being the victims to the equal villany of his son?'

Ines looked from one to the other in bewilderment, then casting herself upon her knees, clasped the thin hand of the old man, exclaiming:

'Ah! is it—can it be possible?'

Don Juan drew her towards him, and placing both hands on her head, his lips moved in blessing, though no sound issued from them. Fear of overtasking the old man's strength, soon caused the friends to leave his bed-side, and he sunk into a quiet sleep.

CHAPTER XV.

*Thus ambition grasps
The empire of the soul; thus pale revenge
Unsheathes her murderous dagger.*—AKENSIDE.

A FEW hours after, Don Carlos, Clifton and Henri were sitting by Pedro's bed-side. He had fallen into a kind of stupor, which lasted several hours; and upon rousing from that, he felt that he was fast failing, and called the friends to listen to his last confession. Turning to Henri, he said, in a feeble voice:

'I have been the *unwilling* instrument of inflicting the deepest wrong upon you. You have supposed yourself the child of a man who, even in your menial situation, was a disgrace to you; but it is not so. Your father was a gentleman of high birth, and heir to extensive wealth. You were stolen from him when too young to remember your parents, by Senor Zenovia.'

The gentlemen started in surprise.

'Stolen by Zenovia!' cried Don Carlos. 'Is it *possible*? But why should I doubt it? From late disclosures, it is proved that his life has been passed in acts of villany. My dear Henri, I congratulate you.'

'Thank you, dear senor; but let us listen to Pedro, while he is able to speak. O, Pedro, tell me quick—do not delay.'

The old man sighed deeply.

'Many years ago,' he commenced, 'I accompanied Senor de Zenovia (who was then a widower) abroad, as his servant. In France he fell violently in love with a young lady, who was engaged to a young Frenchman. My master was madly in love with her; and when she refused him, and married the French gentleman, he raged for a while like a maniac; vowing vengeance upon them both. At last, however, he came home here, leaving a man, whom he paid heavily, to give him every information relative to the objects of his hatred.

'Some four years after this, he visited France again, and found that the young gentleman had just left home for India, to receive a large fortune, which was left to him there. The news soon came that the vessel in which he sailed was lost, and my master carried the intelligence to his wife. She was sick for a long time after it, but at last recovered. Senor Zenovia was at her house a great deal, and pretended to be very friendly. He had found by some means that the lady's husband was not dead, and he intercepted several letters from him; but he continued to talk to the lady of his death.

'After some months passed away, Senor Zenovia asked the lady to marry him, and come over to America; but she would not consent, and said something that made him furious. He gave her the letters from her husband, but told her he would have revenge. He gave the husband of the child's nurse a heavy sum to let him take the child; and in the absence of his honest nurse, I took the boy, and brought him to Senor Zenovia, who brought him away with him, and kept him in his own house for several years. He was the perfect image of his father, and my master hated him and treated him very harshly. At last he gave him to Senor de Montaldo, to bring up as one of his lowest servants, making up a falsehood to account for his having the boy.

'My master was always angry because he was well treated here; but he had given him away and could not prevent it. He told me to change his name, but the poor child would answer to nothing but Henri, and I told my master I would never force another name upon him. Believe me,' he said, turning to Henri, 'I have been miserable, when I have thought of how much I had done to injure you,' and he paused.

'But the name,' cried Henri; 'my father's name—is it the same that I bear?'

'No,' replied the old man; 'your father was Compte de Morinval, and your grandfather Marquis de la Croisy, of Rouen.'

Henri bowed his head upon his hand, and for a long time remained silent; at last he took the hand of Don Carlos, exclaiming:

'O, my dear senor, you have been a father to me indeed, rather than a master, who might have claimed the most rigorous servitude; and if I ever find my parents (which I fear is scarcely probable), they will bless you for your attention to their child.'

Pedro looked at him wistfully; several times he attempted to speak, and at last he said:

'Will you not forgive me? I am dying, and would wish to die in peace.'

Henry extended his hand—

'Yes, I forgive you,' he said, 'and if you sincerely repent, may God also pardon you, even at the hour of death.'

The friends now separated. Clifton joined his command, and Don Carlos visited Zenovia. As he entered, the latter turned away coloring with shame and rage. Don Carlos advanced to his side, and addressed him, calmly:

'Senor Zenovia,' he said, 'you of course have relinquished all idea of obtaining the hand of my daughter. I could never receive for a son a man guilty of such crimes as you have committed; even if the base attempt upon herself had not forever rendered that impossible. Pedro is about dying, and has confessed the numerous atrocities which together you have perpetrated. The history of Henri Duvalle has been repeated. My poor father has been found, and released from a loathsome dungeon, when left by you to perish by a lingering death. He has been saved by Captain Clifton, the affianced husband of Ines, that noble being whom you plotted to murder in his prison.

'I have already sent to the authorities an account of your conduct, and very soon you will be summoned to accompany them where due justice will be meted out to you. I forbear reproach, Senor Zenovia. I think your conscience will reprove you sufficiently. God has in his justice brought your iniquity to light, and saved the innocent from perishing through your villany, and I am thankful.'

As he ceased speaking, Don Carlos turned and left the room, with a charge to the guard to look well to their prisoner.

Rage, hatred, fear—the idea of an ignominious death, which he could not escape, rendered Zenovia almost beside himself.—Half delirious with so many mingled emotions, he sat, his hands clenched, and his eyes rolling with horror for a moment; then suddenly starting up, he bounded to the side of one of his guard, and before he was aware of his intention, snatched a dagger from his belt and plunged it into his own bosom. His momentary delirium gave him the courage that otherwise he could not have summoned. A wild commotion within the room reached the ear of Don Carlos before he had advanced many paces, and he stepped back. There lay Zenovia, weltering in a pool of blood drawn from his own heart. His eyes rolled wildly in his head for a moment; a convulsive shudder ran through his frame, and his guilty soul fled, uncalled for, to the presence of his Creator.

Don Carlos knelt and prayed fervently for the pardon of the soul just departed its earthly tenement. The American guard did not, of course, believe in the efficacy of prayer for the dead, but struck with awe, they looked on in silence. A few moments after, the government officers entered the room for their prisoner. The circumstances were explained, and Zenovia was by them removed for interment. The five prisoners taken with him were placed in their charge, and they departed. Pedro died before night—a Catholic *padre* was with him—gave him absolution; and he died in peace.

The events of the last two or three days cast a gloom over the house for a time; but soon things resumed their usual course. Clifton spent most of his time at Senor de Montaldo's. He was happy now, and he saw the same sentiment in the bright eyes of his sweet Ines.

Stanley called often, and his affectionate heart truly sympathized in his friend's felicity. The commander-in-chief placed officers over the city, and made every arrangement for the security of his army with his usual prudence and foresight. Soon after the city came into their possession, letters arrived from the States to our friends. Clifton received one from his mother, in which she said her health was very poor, and urged him, if it was consistent, to leave the army and come home to her. She described her lonely hours in his absence, and trusted his affection, as well as his duty, would lead him home. He also received a letter from Mr. Hereford, containing a sketch of what Monsieur Dupage had related to him, and ended thus:

'From your description of the young Henri mentioned in your letter, I must hope that he is indeed the lost son of my dear friend; but I dare not impart my suspicions to him, as I would not wish to raise false hopes. You will probably soon return—at least I hope so; and can you not bring Henri with you? I am impatient to see the father and son united. Alphonso is with us; at least, what time he can spare from his visits at your mother's.'

Arthur read this last sentence with a smile. 'Ah,' thought he, 'has my lovely Helen, then, brought the gay Montaldo to her feet? That is pleasant news, if true.'

Don Carlos now entered, and advancing, said:

'Well, Clifton, I have a letter here from Alphonso. He has been falling in love with one of your mother's ladies, and here asks my consent to his union. Read this, and tell me if I had better grant his wishes.'

Arthur perused, and returned the letter with a bright smile.

'My cousin Helen,' he answered, 'is very dear to me. I do not like the idea of giving her up, and I know of no one but your son on whom I would bestow her.'

'I certainly have no reason to dispute her worth,' said Don Carlos, laughing, 'judging by what I know of one nearly related to her. My happiness lies in that of my children, and I shall not oppose my son in what I am convinced will increase his happiness.'

Arthur now communicated the contents of his letters, and saying he should resign his commission immediately, gained permission from Don Carlos to make Ines the companion of his journey home. After a short silence, Don Carlos said:

'My friend, in giving you my daughter, I give you a treasure in herself, but her fortune, I regret to say, is very trifling. I have lost much, very much, during the prosecution of this war, so that I am nearly robbed of resources; but if I have read your heart aright, that will not change your sentiments towards Ines.'

'You have indeed read it aright,' replied Clifton. 'My fortune is sufficient to surround us with every luxury, and her dear, lovely self is all I desire; believe me, my friend, I do not in the least regret it;' and his eyes sparkling with pleasure evinced his truth.

Clifton immediately sent letters to the States, informing his friends of the events which had taken place in Mexico. He requested Mr. Hereford to meet him at Vera Cruz, with a clergyman from New Orleans, to unite him forever to the beloved of his heart. He wrote, also, of the disclosures in regard to Henri, and requested him to bring Monsieur Dupage to Vera Cruz, but without telling him the reality, as he wished to see if there was any natural sympathy between the father and son, which would lead them instinctively to each other. Ines also wrote at the same time to Alice Hereford.

The commander-in-chief accepted the resignation of Clifton; and Stanley and they were very busy in making arrangements for their journey home. The last of October a train was to start for Vera Cruz, and our friends were to travel under protection of its escort.

Don Juan de Montaldo had recovered his strength and a degree of health; he was serene and happy in the society of his recovered friends, who watched over him with the tenderest care. About a week before the time appointed to leave Mexico, Stanley received a letter by the English courier, which caused him much agitation. Rushing to his friend, he said:

'Here, my friend, have I not reason to be thankful? Read this.'

It was from the attorney, whose absence he had lamented, on his return from Europe. We will give some extracts of the letter, as the easiest way to inform our readers of the facts relating to Stanley's loss of fortune. He commenced:

'At last, my friend Edward, I have found a trace of you. I have searched the old world, and at least a part of the new, and have just succeeded in tracing you with the besieging army in Mexico. As soon as this reaches you, if it is possible, return home. I say *home*, my friend, for you are NOT the friendless, isolated being you doubtless imagine yourself; but to explain.

'When you left home for Europe, you know your father, Mr. Melmoth, had married a woman who excited your dislike so much that you expressed it to me. She has proved far worse than you could imagine. About a year before the death of Mr. Melmoth, I perceived that he began to grow melancholy, and sometimes presumed upon my long friendship to question him as to its cause; but he would always wave the subject. At last I found a clue to his sadness. Reports began to circulate that his wife was more intimate with her *brother* than their relationship warranted; and it was even whispered that he was not a brother, but a LOVER, who shared more of her affection than was compatible with her duty to her husband. Then I did not wonder at my friend's sadness; only thinking strange that he did not cast them both off at once.

'Some three weeks previous to his death I called upon him, but was told by his servant that he would receive no company. I told him to take in my name, and I knew he would admit his old friend. He pretended to obey my orders, and returning, said his master wished to be excused to-day. I went home surprised and very much grieved.

'A week passed by, and I heard many of his old friends complain of the same treatment; and to some of them the servants intimated that their master had been drinking deeply, and did not like to be seen. At the close of a week, I again went to his home and solicited admission. This time his wife met me, and in answer to my request, said her husband was not in a state to see company. I immediately demanded the reason. She said in a low voice, affecting to be very much mortified, that he had become a perfect inebriate—that he was almost constantly in a state so degrading, that she could not think of admitting any one to his room. In vain I urged. She was obstinate; and I was forced to return home, chagrined at my want of success. But I could not be contented. I did not—I could not believe what she said, for I had always thought him too high-minded to stoop so low, and I determined to try again. Proceeding there quite early one morning, while they were breakfasting—I did not ring at the door, but opened it, and made my way alone to my friend's room, fortunately without meeting any person. Mr. Melmoth was in bed, pale and emaciated. He attempted to rise, but could scarcely support himself. As I entered, he held out his hand and looked eagerly at me—

'"O," he cried, "how did you pass my jailors? But turn the key in the lock before you answer me."

'I obeyed him; and taking a seat by his side, told him how I had been refused admittance, and at last found my way there entirely alone.

'"And doubtless you have heard, too, that I was intoxicated, and received no company, have you not?"

'I bowed without reply.

'"But you did not believe it?" he cried, lookingly earnestly in my face. "Ah, no! I know you did not."

'I assured him that I knew him too well for that. He pressed my hand, and after a pause of a moment, he said:

'"I am glad you have come. I feel that I am dying, and wish to tell you something concerning my family. Take a pencil and note it down. My friend," he continued, glancing around the room, "they are killing me—my wife and her pretended brother. I have no proof, but I believe it; I am taking slow poison."

'Then why do you stay here? Why not at once denounce them to justice? interrupting him.

'"Surely," he replied, "am I not kept a close prisoner—all my friends denied admission to my presence? and now it is too late! I am dying. But listen to me: they are doing this for my property; they wish to secure ALL to themselves, and will not stop here. My children, I fear, will fall a sacrifice to their cupidity. O, to *you* I look to warn and protect them.

'"While a widower, you drew up for me a will in favor of my three children. It has been recorded, and cannot be disputed. It is there," pointing to a cabinet; "touch that secret spring: now place the will in your bosom. My wife has urged me for a long time to make one in her favor, and has even threatened that I will be forced to do it; but remember what I say to you, *that* is my will, and I shall *never* make another.

'"That *brother*, or rather *paramour*, of my wife," he cried, bitterly, "I have forbidden the house, but she still acts under his direction. Now, my friend, you must go, or they will surprise you here. Do not forget my *children*. If you choose, return to-night with authority to open this house, and take me hence. I have little anxiety about it myself."

'He pressed my hand, and softly unlocking the door, I went out.

'As I closed the hall door and walked rapidly down the street, I saw one of the servants looking after me, and knew that I was discovered. I returned at night, as I had promised, but Mr. Melmoth was dead. There was no proof of foul play, and so the guilty ones escaped. I resolved to wait and see what course the widow would pursue, before I made known the affair of the will.

'At this time I was taken violently ill, and

it was two weeks before I was able to go out. Then I found that your brother, Francis, had returned home a week before, and was now an inmate of that house of mystery. I hastened there, and was told he was not at home. The next morning I called again, and was received by your father's widow. She told me very politely that her son was very sick, having been taken in a fit the night previous, but she would conduct me to him.

'Her frank, open manner staggered my opinion of her guilt for a moment. Your brother lay upon his couch, insensible. A respectable physician of the city sat by his side. I asked his opinion of his patient. He shook his head—said he feared he would never be any better, but he would do all in his power for him. The doctor left with me. I asked him if he had any suspicions that our young friend came to his illness by unfair means.

'"O, I think not," was his answer; "I have discovered nothing of the kind."

'Still I was not satisfied, and determined to visit him, unknown to the family. This I accomplished the next evening. Francis was perfectly sensible, but a mere shadow of what he had been. He seemed exceedingly glad to see me.

'What, my poor boy,' I cried, 'what has brought you to this?'

'He sighed deeply.

'"My health has not been very good for some time past," he answered, "and when I returned home, and found that my father was dead, and his wife told me such dreadful stories of his late conduct, I could not believe them, certainly; but my bereavement was sudden, and I sunk under the shock. I was placed upon a couch, and have not since left it. You know, of course," turning to me, "that my father has made a will entirely in favor of his wife. I have heard it read, and cannot dispute it, though it seems cruel."

'Your father never made that will,' I replied. I then repeated my conversation with Mr. Melmoth.

'"O, this is horrible!" he cried, wringing his hands in agony, "and I too am probably their victim. Last night I heard my father's wife speaking in low tones to the man she has so long called her brother, but who is now her husband. They thought me insensible, but I was listening. I heard her say, "We will soon have Francis with his father and sister, and then everything will be ours; by this I think they are helping me out of the world."

'After a moment's pause to take breath, he continued: "My friend, sit down and listen to me for a few moments. I have been absent several years at college, and know but little of what passed at home. Some three weeks since, I received a visit from *her brother*." He lowered his voice. "He brought me a letter from my father, in which he wrote, that my brother Edward was dead; and he requested me, as I valued his blessing, to go to the bank and draw my brother's patrimony in his name, and come home to him, as he was very feeble. He enjoined it upon me repeatedly to fulfil his wishes. I was surprised—for it seemed a strange proceeding—but as my brother was dead, and my father commanded, I obeyed. When I returned home, I found my father had died before the letter was written—and when I charged his wife with it she looked too guilty to remove my suspicions."

'You are right,' I interrupted, 'your father never wrote to you in that way, he was too upright—besides, your brother is not dead. Here is a letter I received from him but yesterday; he is well, but anxious about his friends at home, as he has not heard from you in many months.'

Francis clasped his hands. "O, indeed that is happy tidings," he cried. "There, quick, quick, my friend, in the secret drawer in yonder cabinet, you will find what I drew from security. It is all safe! Take it, conceal it about you—and when Edward comes, give him the amount, and ask him to forgive me. I have done wrong, though I knew it not at the time."

' I promised all he wished.

' "They have been searching several days for the money you now have, but there they shall be disappointed. Through their imposition, I was betrayed into taking it, but they shall never reap the benefit they looked for; and now, too, they report that I have spent my time for months at low gambling houses. O, my friend, I look to *you* to clear my fame, and that of my father and dear Edward. O, keep them out of their clutches, promise me that you will."

' I promised all he desired, and asked if he would not allow me to remove him from the house.

' "O no," he cried, " it is useless. I cannot survive more than a day or two, they have taken good care of that." As we parted, he pressed my hand to his heart. " Farewell!" he cried, " I shall never see you again !"

' He said too true, for he died before morning. Scarcely an hour after I heard of his death I was again seized with that painful malady which has so many times threatened my life. My physician told me I must leave the country in less than twenty-four hours—that I must travel for months, it was the only thing that would keep me from the grave. I related to him the circumstances I am now writing to you, and protested I must stay to bring the offenders to justice. He however advised me to seek you, accompany you home, and then together prosecute the affair in hand. I set out the next day, and in reaching Florence, where your last letter was dated, found you had long since left for home. This was a disappointment. My health would not permit my immediate return, and I wrote to you, but suppose you never received the communication. Two months since, I returned home, you were not to be found, though I made every inquiry for you.

' I immediately commenced a prosecution against your father's widow and her husband, Mr. Windsor, for forgery. They were living in high style in Mr. Melmoth's house. I learned upon inquiry, that he had formerly kept one of the lowest gambling houses in the city. I called upon Mrs. Windsor, and requested her to vacate the house, and also relinquish all right to any part of Mr. Melmoth's property, as his will was made entirely in favor of his children. She answered with the utmost effrontery, that by her husband's last will, executed three days before his death, he had given her all he possessed. I called for the will and found it in due form, as she had said. Taking the names of the attorney and witnesses, I after much trouble ferreted them out. The two witnesses I found at last, in one of the *hells* with which our town is disgraced. They were of the very lowest class of human beings. It was some time before we could learn anything from them. At last, by promises that they should not be proceeded against, we succeeded—they confessed that three days after Mr. Melmoth died, Windsor had offered them a large sum of money to witness a will which he said Mr. Melmoth had signed, but died so suddenly that witnesses had not been called. They said Windsor, his wife, and the attorney were present at the time. Their deposition was taken down, and themselves placed in durance till called for. Next, the servants were examined, and being threatened with punishment in case of obstinacy, said that they had been bribed by their mistress to utter falsehoods, in order to blacken the character of their master and his son, and they had never seen the least thing in either but was perfectly fair and honorable.

' With this array of proof, we had only to go forward. The attorney who drew up the will, fled from the country, and we have not been able to trace him. Windsor and his wife were thrown into prison, and when they found their guilt proved beyond doubt, and disgrace and punishment would ensue, the hero of the drama strangled himself with his handkerchief, while his wife, oppressed with terror of her approaching fate, and perhaps with remorse for her guilty life, is now a raging maniac, kept in close confinement in an asylum. Everything is now clear, my dear Edward. You must return and resume your station in the world. By the conditions of the will, on the death of your brother and sister, you are Mr. Melmoth's sole heir. I congratulate you, Edward. I know your proud spirit, and am certain you must have suffered much; but I hope the future will amply compensate for the past.'

As Clifton closed this long epistle, he turned to his friend with a glance that revealed all the glad feelings of his soul. 'Ah, my friend,' he cried, 'you can scarcely be more rejoiced at this change than myself.'

Stanley pressed his friend's hand in silence. His heart was overflowing with too many different emotions to allow him the power of speech. We will not aver, that some thought of Alice Hereford did not mingle with his pleasurable emotions.

The next week the train left Mexico for Vera Cruz, and with it our small company, Don Carlos, his daughter, and Henri—with Clifton, and Stanley, bade adieu to their friends—Don Juan blessing his grandchild and her young lover, and commending them to the care of Heaven.

CHAPTER XVI.

Which crowns the bliss of two hearts, and brings others nearer to a happy issue.

'Mirth, music, friendship, love's propitious smile,
Chase every care.'

It was towards evening, on a bright day about the middle of November, that a body of American troops rode forth from the city of Vera Cruz, to meet a train just approaching from the city of Mexico. The advance was already seen at a distance, their banners streaming forth in the sunlight; while enlivening strains of music floated upon the air. On a piazza of one of the first hotels, might be seen a small party standing in a group, apart from the crowd. The entrance of the train seemed to occupy their attention exclusively. There they stood, making comments upon the different heroes as they passed. After a while, exclamations of impatience escaped some of the party. 'Will they *never* come?' cried a lively girl, who was bending over and examining the faces of those passing in the street below. 'What do you think?' she continued, turning and addressing a young gentleman by her side. 'Do you think they have decided to take up their residence in Mexico?'

'Perhaps so,' he answered with a smile; the next moment he exclaimed, ' who do you think that carriage contains? Do you recognize any one there, Mademoiselle Marie?'

'Ah, there they are, sure enough; but look, Senor Alphonso, they do not deign us even a glance—they are, going to the house across the way. There is Arthur and his friend riding by the carriage. But do you know the gentleman with your sister Ines?'

'The elder,' replied Alphonso, 'is my father—the other, an adopted brother; but they have alighted, and are disappearing within. My friends, you will excuse me, if I leave you a few moments.'

He darted away, and in a few moments was seen entering, where his friends had disappeared.

Mr. Hereford and Monsieur De la Croisy, with their daughters, composed the party we have mentioned. They remained at their station but a few moments, and then retired within. In a short time Alphonso returned, and introduced his friends into a large private room, which Mr. Hereford had secured for the party. We will pass over the joyful meeting of the re-united friends, leaving it to the imagination of the reader. Clifton was quite disappointed that Helen was not present. Alphonso told him 'that his mother was rather feeble, and her daughter could not think of leaving her.'

Stanley now did not attempt to veil his sentiments for Miss Hereford. Love spoke in every glance. Her eyes fell before his own, with a soft confusion, which awakened fervent hope in his bosom, an inmate rarely occupying that sanctum. After the first greetings were over, and the feelings of the company had subsided into something like calmness, Clifton at a glance from Mr. Hereford, left the room, and in a moment returned with Henri, whispering to him as he entered, to be composed and not betray himself by his agitation.

Arthur first presented him to Mr. Hereford and Alice—and then led him to Monsieur De la Croisy, with the introduction—'Senor De Montaldo's adopted son, and my preserver from a prison and death.' The doctor arose, extended his hand with a smile of welcome, and leading him to Marie, introduced his daughter. He stood for a moment, with the hand of each in his own, unmindful of the singularity of his manner. He gazed from Henri to Marie, and then again his eyes were rivetted upon the young man's face—while an expression of strange bewilderment crossed his features.

Henri dared not raise his eyes, but turned away fearful of betraying his agitation. Suddenly the doctor dropped the hands he had hitherto held firmly—and commenced pacing the room rapidly.

Henri took a seat by Marie, and tried to converse with her, but he was agitated in spite of himself, and his eyes continually wandered to his father—he longed to kneel at his feet, and ask his blessing.

Marie following his wandering glances, said: 'My dear father seems strangely affected from meeting you to night.'

Henri raised his eyes at the moment, and met those of his father, fastened upon his face.

The doctor darted forward, and seizing the other's hand, cried in a voice hoarse with emotion, 'Who are you?—What are you?—Those eyes!—O! once they looked into mine with love and tenderness. Whose are they—tell me?' He seemed almost wild in his eagerness.

Henri, no longer able to control his emotion, cast himself at his father's feet. 'Those eyes,' he cried, 'will ever look with the warmest affection upon Monsieur De la Croisy.'

The doctor sunk upon his knees. 'Henri.'

'My father.'

They were in each other's arms sobbing like children.

Marie threw her arms around her recovered brother's neck—and her ever bright face was bedewed with warm tears. Not an eye in the room but was humid from sympathy. *Reader*, allow us to drop the curtain!

The next morning, a small but happy company were assembled in one of the parlors of the hotel. The party of the evening before was increased by two or three American officers, and as many ladies of the town. The young people were gay, and in vivid spirits. The elder gentlemen were happy in the remembrance of their own youthful days. The whole countenance of M. De la Croisy beamed with joyful emotion, as he gazed on his new found son and lively daughter; and he looked forward to a serene decline of life, spent in the society of his children.

There was a momentary hush—a door opened—a lady and gentleman advanced to the centre of the room. Stanley led Miss Hereford to the lady's side, and himself retreated to his friend's right hand. The clergyman in his robes approached to join two loving hearts in the secret bonds of everlasting union. Don Carlos gave the bride away with a swelling heart—and Clifton, as he pressed the golden circlet upon her finger, and clasped her to his bosom, softly whispered—

'Thus let me hold thee to my heart,
And every care resign;
And shall we never—never part,
O! thou my all that's mine!'

The ceremony and congratulations over, they repaired to another room, where by direction of the bridegroom, an elegant repast was laid out. Rare exotics, shed a grateful fragrance through the room; while soft strains of melting harmony, from unseen minstrels, stole over them, seeming to enchain the soul, and 'wrap it in elysium.'

The bridal party remained several days in Vera Cruz, and then came the parting.

The idea of saying adieu to his daughter was very bitter to Don Carlos, but he checked his regrets. He saw she had given her young heart in all its freshness and purity, to one every way worthy of her—and who returned her affection, by an ardent devotion which could not fail to make her happy. As she clung weeping to his bosom, though scarcely able to control his own feelings, he endeavored to cheer her. She at last raised her head, and said in a trembling voice: 'My dearest father, though I leave you now, I shall very often visit you, in your own lonely home; and I do not leave you entirely alone. You have dear grandfather with you; and Alphonso, with his bride, will soon meet you in Mexico.

Clifton now advanced, and received his trembling bride in his arms, while Don Carlos turned to say farewell to his son. He granted Alphonso a willing consent to the completion of his wishes—and obtained a promise, that as soon as the affairs in Mexico had become settled, he would take his bride home.

Monsieur De la Croisy repeatedly expressed his heart-felt gratitude to Senor De Montaldo, for the parental care and attention he had bestowed upon his child—and at parting, pressed upon his acceptance, the sum of 100,000 dollars. Don Carlos for a long time refused to accept it.

'Do not grieve me by a refusal,' cried De Croisy. 'I do not offer this merely in payment for what you have expended upon Henri; but I trust you will accept it as a token of gratitude and esteem, for the parental affection you have extended to my son, when his father was debarred the privilege ever of knowing that he lived.'

Don Carlos now turned to Henri. 'My young friend,' he said, 'believe me, I sincerely rejoice in your prospects of future happiness. You have found an affectionate parent, and lovely sister, who meet even your most exalted hopes. I trust, in your accession to rank and wealth, the friends of your youth will not be forgotten.'

'O, never, my more than parent!' cried Henri, with emotion, '*never* will I forget those who have supplied the place of my natural protectors—never cease to remember them with prayers for their safety and happiness.'

The hour is past! the vessel has left the shore—and the sad Don Carlos is left to return to his lonely home.

Soon our little party reached New Orleans —and were received with a rapturous welcome, by their affectionate friends. Clifton presented his lovely bride to his mother, who, as she enfolded her in a warm embrace, whispered,—'Receive in me a second mother, one to replace *her* you have lost, and who will endeavor to make her Arthur's treasure happy in her new home. Ines now turned to Helen, who had just given Clifton a tender embrace. 'My dear, sweet sister,' exclaimed Helen, 'your return with our truant Arthur, will make us completely happy, and we shall take good care, that you do not leave us soon again.'

'But may we not soon lose *you?*' replied Ines, with an arch smile.

A soft blush suffused Helen's cheek.

'O no! not lose me,' she said, 'we shall be connected by a tie still nearer and dearer than at present.'

In the course of a few days, Stanley not only received his own fortune, but was acknowledged heir of all Mr. Melmoth's vast possessions, and received the congratulations of his friends. The same day, he visited Clifton. His eyes beamed more brightly than usual—a sweet smile played over his lips—and his whole countenance sparkled with animation. He pressed Arthur's hand in his own. 'Now,' he cried, 'I hope to be as happy as my friend; the lovely Alice has consented to secure my felicity, by uniting her fate with mine. After regarding her so long with a hopeless worship, I am soon to be elevated with perfect bliss. Do you not wish me joy?'

'I do indeed, Edward,' replied his friend, 'I wish you as much felicity as I enjoy; more I could not ask for you.'

* * * * *

CHAPTER XVII.

Happiness triumphant. Winding up of the plot, and leave-taking of the reader.

'I stood by the towers of Ardenville,
And the bells rang out a merry peal;
There was a priest in his robes of white,
There was a maiden lovely and bright;
A gallant knight stood by her side,
And the shout of joy sounded far and wide.'

The first day of the new year has come. The city is a scene of gay confusion—the streets are thronged with light-hearted beings on the wing for pleasure.

The bells of Grace Church rang forth their merriest peals upon the clear air. A gay throng magnificently dressed, were pouring into the church by the various avenues. The city clock tolled the hour of two—there was a hush over the brilliant assembly, as the clergyman in his surplice entered the chancel, and knelt for a moment in silent prayer. The deep toned organ sent forth peals of exquisite harmony, as a bridal party ascended the broad aisle, and knelt at the altar. The *two* lovely brides were richly dressed in lace and pearly satin. Their heads were uncovered, save a snowy veil of rich Brussels, fastened in their flowing tresses, and floating back over their graceful shoulders.

Stanley and Alice were first united in the holiest of all relations; Mr. Hereford giving the bride away. Then Clifton advanced, and taking the hand of the rich heiress of Douglass, placed it in that of Montaldo, and the sacred words were pronounced which made them one.

Again the organ poured forth its notes of celestial melody, and the party moved slowly away. The assemblage present were invited guests—and all now repaired to Mr. Stanley's elegant mansion, to partake of a nuptial feast—everything relating to it was so exquisitely arranged, as to please the most fastidious taste. The rich—the gay—the talented—manly beauty, and female loveliness, mingled in one stream of delighted enjoyment.

Dear reader, we have followed our *friends* through many scenes—have been present at their nuptials—and have pronounced them happy; and now we will close, by a brief mention of some of our principal characters.

Arthur Clifton remains in the city through the winter months, where his young bride attracts universal admiration, and then will return to spend his summers at La Grange Villa, where in the society of his mother, and his sweet Ines, he is confident of enjoying the purest felicity.

Alphonso and Helen will remain with Clifton, till peace is proclaimed in Mexico, when they will depart for his distant home, with the promise, however, of spending part of every year, with their friends here.

Stanley's fascinating bride reigns one of the brightest stars in the galaxy of fashion; but her most absolute dominion is in her husband's heart.

The Marquis De la Croisy, with his recovered son, and the interesting Marie, remained to see their friends united in the bonds of matrimony—and then, with an affectionate adieu, set sail for 'La belle France,' to resume their rank and station, so long thrown aside.

Having now brought our *friends* to the acme of earthly felicity, we will leave them to pursue their course through the world, grateful for the blessings of the past, and hopefully trusting for the future.

THE END.